Frederick William Farrar

Non-Biblical systems of religion : a symposium

Frederick William Farrar

Non-Biblical systems of religion : a symposium

ISBN/EAN: 9783337261573

Printed in Europe, USA, Canada, Australia, Japan

Cover: Foto ©Lupo / pixelio.de

More available books at **www.hansebooks.com**

Nisbet's Theological Library.

SYMPOSIUMS

ON

GREAT QUESTIONS IN THEOLOGY AND LIFE.

Uniform style, 12mo, cloth, $1.50 each.

CHRISTIANITY AND EVOLUTION; or, Modern Problems of the Faith. By Various Writers.

NON-BIBLICAL SYSTEMS OF RELIGION: A Symposium. By the Ven. Archdeacon FARRAR, D.D., Rev. Canon RAWLINSON, M.A., Rev. W. WRIGHT, D.D., Rabbi G. J. EMANUEL, B.A., Sir WILLIAM MUIR, Rev. EDWIN JOHNSON, M.A., T. W. RHYS DAVIDS, LL.D., Ph.D., the Hon. RASMUS B. ANDERSON, Rev. W. NICOLSON, M.A.

FUTURE PROBATION: A Symposium on the Question, "Is Salvation Possible after Death?" By the Rev. STANLEY LEATHES, D.D., Principal J. CAIRNS, D.D., LL.D., Rev. EDWARD WHITE, Rev. STOPFORD BROOKE, M.A., Rev. Dr. LITTLEDALE, Right Rev. the BISHOP OF AMYCLA, &c.

IMMORTALITY: A Symposium on What are the Foundations of the Belief in the Immortality of Man? By the Rev. Prebendary Row, M.A., Rabbi HERMANN ADLER, Professor G. G. STOKES, F.R.S., Rev. Canon KNOX-LITTLE, Right Rev. BISHOP OF AMYCLA, Rev. JOHN CAIRNS, D.D., Rev. EDWARD WHITE, and others.

THE ATONEMENT: A Symposium. By Archdeacon FARRAR, Professor ISRAEL ABRAHAMS, Rev. Dr. LITTLEDALE, Rev. G. W. OLVER, Principal RAINY, D.D., the BISHOP OF AMYCLA, and others.

INSPIRATION: A Symposium on In what Sense and within what Limits is the Bible the Word of God? By Archdeacon FARRAR, the Revs. Principal CAIRNS, STANLEY LEATHES, D.D., Prebendary Row, J. RADFORD THOMSON, Right Rev. BISHOP OF AMYCLA, and others.

NEW YORK:

THOMAS WHITTAKER, 2 AND 3 BIBLE HOUSE.

Non-Biblical Systems of Religion.

A Symposium.

BY THE

VEN. ARCHDEACON FARRAR, D.D.,
REV. CANON RAWLINSON, M.A.,
REV. W. WRIGHT, D.D.,
RABBI G. J. EMANUEL, B.A.,
SIR WILLIAM MUIR,
REV. EDWIN JOHNSON, M.A.,
T. W. RHYS DAVIDS, LL.D., PH.D.,
THE HON. RASMUS B. ANDERSON,
REV. WM. NICOLSON, M.A.

NEW YORK:
T. WHITTAKER, BIBLE HOUSE.
1887.

PREFACE.

THE following articles are reprinted from the *Homiletic Magazine*. The subject is of such importance that this volume will probably be heartily welcomed by those who are studying Comparative Religionism, the questions connected with which, the recent notable advances of research, and our increasing facilities of intercourse with foreign nations, have brought, in an unmistakable manner, to the front. Our aim has been to furnish comprehensive outlines of the chief religious systems of the world in a popular yet fairly accurate and scholarly way. Many of the writers are recognised authorities in their respective departments. A few heathen systems—*e.g.*, Brahmanism and Zoroastrianism—have not been touched upon, but the sources of information respecting them are both numerous and easy of access. Believing, as we do, that Christianity has nothing to fear, but a great deal to gain, from an intelligent comparison of its claims with those of its predecessors and rivals, we commit the book, with all confidence, to the judgment of the public.

FREDK. HASTINGS,
A. F. MUIR,
Editors of the "Homiletic Magazine."

CONTENTS.

I.

INTRODUCTION—ETHNIC INSPIRATION . . . 1
   By the Ven. ARCHDEACON FARRAR, D.D.

II.

ANCIENT EGYPTIAN SYSTEMS 17
   By the Rev. GEORGE RAWLINSON, M.A., Canon of Canterbury Cathedral.

III.

ANCIENT EGYPTIAN SYSTEMS—*continued* . . 35
   By the Rev. GEORGE RAWLINSON, M.A., Canon of Canterbury Cathedral.

IV.

ANCIENT CANAANITE RELIGIONS . . . 54
   By the Rev. WILLIAM WRIGHT, D.D., Secretary to the British and Foreign Bible Society, and Author of "The Empire of the Hittites," &c.

V.

EARLIER HELLENIC RELIGIONS 69
   By the Rev. EDWIN JOHNSON, M.A., Professor of Classical Literature, New College, London.

VI.

THE JEWISH FAITH 85
   By Rabbi G. J. EMANUEL, B.A., of the Jews' Synagogue, Birmingham.

VII.

ISLAM AND CHRISTIANITY 104
   By Sir WILLIAM MUIR, Principal of Edinburgh University.

VIII.

BUDDHISM AND CHRISTIANITY . . . 115
   By T. W. RHYS DAVIDS, LL.D., Ph.D., Barrister-at-Law, and author of "Buddhism," "The Hibbert Lectures, 1881."

IX.

ANCIENT SCANDINAVIAN RELIGION . . 135
   By the Hon. RASMUS B. ANDERSON, Minister of the United States, Denmark, and Author of "Norse Mythology," "America not Discovered by Columbus," &c.

X.

THE RELIGION OF THE ANCIENT SCANDINAVIANS 153
   By the Hon. RASMUS B. ANDERSON.

XI.

POSITIVISM AS A RELIGION 178
   By the Rev. Professor J. RADFORD THOMSON, M.A., New College, London.

XII.

THE ONE PURELY MORAL RELIGION . . 195

By the Rev. W. Nicolson, M.A., of St. Petersburg, Secretary to the British and Foreign Bible Society's Work in Russia.

XIII.

THE ONE PURELY MORAL RELIGION—*continued* 214

By the Rev. W. Nicolson, M.A.

NON-CHRISTIAN RELIGIONS.

A SYMPOSIUM ON: WHAT IS THE RELATION OF NON-CHRISTIAN SYSTEMS TO BIBLICAL THEOLOGY?

INTRODUCTION—ETHNIC INSPIRATION.

I.

BY THE VEN. ARCHDEACON FARRAR, D.D.

NO one who studies the movements of theological thought can have failed to observe that, of late years, there has been a change of tone in the manner of regarding heathen religions. In past days it was common to speak of them with sweeping denunciation as doctrines of devils unrelieved by any ennobling elements. Since the beginning of this century, and partly, perhaps, in consequence of the influence of Lessing, there has been a tendency to search for the elements of truth which they all contain. Thus Brahmanism, dissevered from its later corruptions, has been examined in the light of the Vedas, and found to embody many noble principles. Buddhism has been studied with profound care, and though it must be freely admitted that it is a religion which is practically without a God, and without any doctrine of conscious immortality, it has yet been seen to be in possession of many deep spiritual truths. Our missionaries have testified that in many instances the lives of Buddhist priests set a conspicuous example of sincerity and purity. When the early Jesuit fathers first came in contact with the institutions of Buddhism, they were startled and even shocked by the close resemblance which they presented to those of Latin Christianity. They could find no other solution of the problem than diabolical caricature. It may be that the resemblance is due in part to the similarity of man's religious needs all over the world, and in part to an early diffusion of Christian thought by Nestorian and other missionaries. There are strong grounds for believing that the points of similarity between the story of Guatama and the records of our Lord in the Gospel of St. John are not purely accidental, and they may have been imported into Eastern life by wandering teachers at an age which nearly touches on the Christian era. On the other hand, we have no reason to reject the main contention of Mr.

Herbert Spencer's new book on ecclesiastical institutions, which is that many of the distinctive truths and practices of the faith are not without their analogue in many other forms of religion. There should be nothing to surprise us in such a fact. The heart and mind of man are the same over all the world, and the instinctive impulses of the human spirit have not been left unguided by the great Father of mankind. Let us again compare the treatment of Mohammedanism by recent writers and by those of an earlier period. Mohammed used always to be spoken of with execration as though he were an incarnation of all wickedness. "Blood-stained fanatic" and "wily impostor" were among the milder objurgations bestowed upon him, while Islam was condemned, without mitigation, as a sink of corruption. Deeper knowledge has shown us that a true picture of this religion of so many millions of our race cannot be painted in colours so entirely black. If we still condemn, we have learnt to do so with more fairness and discrimination. We can see that, among many crimes and vices, the Prophet of Arabia had also some noble qualities, and that the ideal of the true Moslem is very far indeed from being despicable or degraded.

Multifarious as are the elements combined in

Scripture, and many as are the different tones in which it speaks to us, yet even from the Old Testament we might have learnt that there is such a thing as Ethnic inspiration, and that God has not confined to the chosen people either His other gifts or His illuminating grace. More than one fragmentary record of heathen origin has been incorporated into Holy Writ. "The spirit of man," says Solomon, "is the candle of the Lord," and by "man" he did not mean the Jew only. Cyrus was a heathen, a worshipper of the sun, yet the later Isaiah not only speaks of him with profound respect, but even calls him "the Messiah" or "anointed" of the Lord. In the "Wisdom Literature" particularly there is a generous recognition of the endowments which God has bestowed upon various members of our race without distinction of nationality or creed. We still read with pleasure on All Saints' Day the beautiful passage of Ecclesiasticus, "Let us now praise famous men, and our fathers that begat us. The Lord hath wrought great glory by them through his power from the beginning. Such as did bear rule in their kingdoms . . . giving counsel by their understanding and declaring prophecies . . . wise and eloquent in their instructions. Such as found out musical tunes and recited verses in writing, rich men furnished with ability, living peaceably in their habitations." These eloquent teachers and great discoverers were not all of the Hebrew race.

In the New Testament, as we should have expected, this thought of the Fatherhood of God and brotherhood of men, and of the common heritage of the gifts of the Spirit, is still more clearly illustrated. Christ's type of love to our neighbour is the mongrel and despised Samaritan. He says of the heathen centurion, that He had not found so great faith, no, not in Israel. Though he was not sent but to the lost sheep of the House of Israel, He extended His miraculous blessings even to the poor Syro-Phœnician woman. His last message to His Apostles was that they were to go into all the world and make disciples of every nation.

Very early did they fulfil the mission. When Peter opened to the Gentiles the gates of the kingdom of Heaven, the Holy Spirit fell on the Roman centurion and his household even before they had been baptized. Philip readily admitted into the Church the Ethiopian eunuch. The Christians who were scattered after the martyrdom of Stephen preached as freely to Greeks as to Jews. Paul and Barnabas devoted themselves mainly to the Apostolate of the Gentiles.

And of all the Apostles, none admitted so fully

as St. Paul the principle of Ethnic inspiration, and the free equal love of God to the heathen as to the Hebrews. His large heart seemed to delight in the prospect of a whole world equally guilty yet equally redeemed. The cosmopolitan sympathies, which may have been due in part to his early Tarsian education, burst into full blossom when they had been transplanted from the barren soil of Pharisaism. In his speech at Lystra he makes a direct appeal to the sense of God's presence as revealed by the beauty and fruitfulness of the natural world. The thought must have been familiar to him from the Book of Wisdom. There, though the heathen are blamed for worshipping "fire, or wind, or the swift air, or the circle of the stars, or the violent water, or the lights of heaven," they are yet partially excused "because the things that are seen are beautiful." They are reminded that if their error arose while peradventure they were seeking God, and desirous to find Him, it would not have been beyond their capacity to infer proportionally from the greatness and beauty of the creatures, "how much mightier is He that made them." * So St. Paul tells the Lystrenians that they should turn from their imaginary gods "unto the living God, who made heaven, and earth,

* Wisdom xiii. 1–9.

and the sea, and all things that are therein; who in times past suffered all nations to walk in their own ways. Nevertheless He left not Himself without witness, in that He did good, and gave rain from heaven, and fruitful seasons, filling our hearts with food and gladness."

With a skill and eloquence yet more remarkable did St. Paul make use of his accidental notice of an altar "to the unknown God" at Athens. He won the attention of the Athenians by telling them that he was but making known to them the God whom, without knowing it, they worshipped. In this speech occurs the noble passage which presents us with his philosophy of history. God—so he tells the Athenian philosophers—had made all the nations of one, and determined their destinies and the bounds of their habitations expressly that they should seek God, if haply they might feel after Him and find Him, though He be not far from every one of us: "For in Him we live and move and have our being, as certain also of your own poets have said, 'For we are also His offspring.'"

Nor was this a mere passing thought with the great Apostle. In the elaborate argument with which he opens his greatest epistle, he contends that it was fully within the power of the heathen to have recognised that which may be known of

God, "for God manifested it unto them. For the invisible things of Him since the creation of the world are clearly seen, being perceived through the things that are made, even His everlasting power and divinity; that they may be without excuse, because that knowing God, they glorified Him not as God, neither gave thanks." He also insists upon the truths of natural religion when he says that there were Gentiles who, not having the law, did *by nature* the things contained in the law. Thus they were "a law unto themselves," and showed "the work of the law written in their hearts, their conscience also bearing witness, and their thoughts the meanwhile accusing or else excusing one another."

And while St. Paul thus shows his recognition of the elements of a natural religion by this broad and kindly view of God's dealings with the heathen world, he practically illustrates his belief by his obvious sympathy with their institutions and mode of life. The burning hatred of a Jew for every form of idolatry did not prevent him from looking with sympathy on the more innocent aspects of pagan life. He twice derives his metaphors from the theatre,* and frequently from the Greek games—the chariot-race, the boxing-match, the

---

* 1 Cor. iv. 9; vii. 31.

runners and their prize garlands of parsley or of pine.* It is also known to all that he introduces at least three direct quotations from heathen poets into the sacred page. In Titus i. 12 he quotes a famous proverbial hexameter of Epimenides; in 1 Cor. xv. 33 an iambic of Menander; and in his speech on the Areopagus an hemistich which is found both in Kleanthes and Aratus. I have shown elsewhere that each of the three quotations was more or less proverbial; † that each of them occurs in at least two poets; and that taken alone they are wholly insufficient to prove that the Apostle had anything but the most meagre acquaintance with Greek literature. They are the only quotations which he uses, unless the conclusion of the speech at Lystra, which easily falls into an anapæstic rhythm, be also a quotation from some unknown lyric poet. But whether St. Paul had read much Greek literature or not, it is interesting to see that he does not shrink from adducing the thoughts and words of heathen writers not only in addressing idolaters, but even in solemn epistles to Christian men.

And it may, I think, be fairly inferred from

---

* 1 Cor. ix. 24; Phil. iii. 14; 1 Thess. ii. 19; 1 Tim. vi. 12; 2 Tim. iv. 8.

† *Life of St. Paul*, i. 630–633

these arguments and quotations that St. Paul would have been the last to deny that there was such a thing as Ethnic inspiration. Nor would St. James have denied it, though his whole tone of mind was more rigid and Judaic than that of his great contemporary. The hexametrical and iambic rhythms in his epistle may not prove much, and may even be due to a Greek amanuensis; nor can we insist on the classic parallels which may be furnished for several passages in his epistle, nor on the curious expression "the wheel of nature." *
But St. James lays down, without any limitation, the great principle that every good gift ($δόσις$) and every perfect boon ($δώρημα$) is from above, coming down from the Father of lights—"with whom," he adds, apparently with a reference to the discoveries of astronomy, "can be no variation, neither shadow that is cast by turning."

In this principle of St. James we find the strongest recognition of the truth that there can be no power of the human intellect which is not bestowed by God. He must clearly, therefore, have believed that the wisdom, the eloquence, the piety of pagan writers was the result of an inspiration from above.

Nor is St. John less clear in his statement of the

---

* James iii. 6, $τὸν τρόχον τῆς γενέσεως$.

truth that God has revealed Himself to, and has inspired, men in all ages. He dwells on this thought in the golden prologue of his Gospel. The Eternal Word, he says, created all things. "In Him was life, and *the life was the light of men.*" He was manifested in historic presence; He was yet more fully manifested by the outpouring of His Spirit; but He had been manifested by His works from the beginning of the creation, not only to separate individuals, but to man, who, being made in the image of God, stood in a special relation to Him. "He saith not the light *of the Jews only*"—such is the comment of Theophylact—"*but of all men:*" for all of us, so far as we have received intellect and reason from that Word which created us, are said to be illumined by Him. The light of the Divine Word has been shining continuously amid man's self-induced darkness, and deep as that darkness at times became, it never wholly overcame (κατέλαβεν) the heavenly light. Amid many false lights there was always the true light, which in Nature and life and conscience is ever coming into the world, and which leaves no single man wholly destitute of a Divine illumination.* In this profound passage St. John does but clearly express and illustrate what had been implied so long before in the rap-

* John i. 4, 5 9, and Canon Westcott's *Commentary.*

turous exclamation of David, "How excellent is Thy loving-kindness, O God! therefore the children of men put their trust under the shadow of Thy wings. . . . For with Thee is the fountain of life; in Thy light do we see light."*

We are prepared, then, to see the light of God shining even on the heathen. In the sacred books of the East there are many lovely and holy thoughts, many flashes of subtle insight, many trains of profound speculation. The classic writers of Greece and Rome have enriched the thoughts of the world with a literature that has never been surpassed. The attitude of Christians towards this literature has often been singularly narrow and mistaken. They have condemned the study of it as involving a waste of time and a diminution of spirituality. They have failed to see that exquisite thoughts conveyed in perfect language could hardly have been due to an inspiration of the devil. The Emperor Julian showed deeper insight when he saw that Christian teachers gained greatly from the study of pagan literature, and therefore forbad "the Galileans" to avail themselves of this source of culture. He was well aware that among the opponents of the pagan reaction, at the head of which he placed himself, none were so much to be

* Psalm xxxvi. 7–9.

dreaded as the great Cappadocian scholars, Basil the Great and Gregory of Nazianzus, who had been fellow-students with himself in the schools of Athens. It is true that the ascetic spirit was inclined to disparage the study of pagan writers as a waste of time. Jerome in his early years had been an ardent student of classical literature, but his conscience was rendered uneasy by a dream, in which he was suddenly taken before the judgment-seat of God, and there fell on his face in terror. Asked who he was, he replied, "I am a Christian." "Thou liest," was the answer; "thou art a Ciceronian, not a Christian; for where your treasure is, there also is your heart." He was then scourged, and in his agony cried out that he would never again offend by heathen studies. The frequency of the classical allusions in later writings makes it tolerably certain, however, that he could not entirely have abandoned the favourite reading of his earlier days. Indeed, when taunted by Rufinus with having broken his vow, he falls back upon the plea that after all that vow was only taken in a dream. As time went on, the jealousy felt by Christian writers towards grammatic studies became deeper and stronger. Gregory the Great—in terms which at once recall those which Shakespeare puts into the mouth of Jack Cade—severely reproved Didier, Archbishop of Vienne, for trying to reintroduce the teaching of grammar. But the entire abandonment of classical studies synchronised with the period in which mankind fell into the deepest ignorance and subjection. The Revival of Letters led to the revival of a purer Christianity. The Humanists were the immediate precursors of the Reformers. "Greece rose from the dead with the New Testament in her hand."

And if some great Christian teachers—especially among the later and Western Fathers—were inclined to disparage the entire life and thought and literature of the heathen world, we must not forget that the great Greek Fathers showed a wiser liberality. Justin Martyr, who had himself entered Christianity through the portals of Philosophy, held that all who lived conformably to truth were Christians, even if they were regarded as atheists. Among them he mentions Socrates and Heraclitus. He even goes so far as to say that Socrates had known Christ, though only in part, since Christ is the Divine Reason, of whom every race of men partakes.* He also, like other Fathers, attributes inspiration to "The Sibyl" and "Hystaspes," and freely quotes from them. Clement of Alexandria is still more cosmopolitan in his theo-

* Just. Mart. *Apol.*, i. 46, ii. 10.

logy. He had anticipated Lessing by many centuries in his conception of the education of the human race by a Divine Instructor. He does not give any definition of "Inspiration"—indeed no Christian Father has done so, nor has any definition ever been accepted by the Universal Church —but it appears from almost every page of his writings that he drew no distinction in kind between the inspiration of the sacred writers and that which he believed to have been imparted to the greatest of the Greek philosophers. In these views he was heartily followed by Origen and others of the Greek fathers, who believed in the reality of Ethnic inspiration, if by that phrase we mean to imply that some of the greatest and wisest of the heathen not only groped after God, but really found Him,—that they were sincere in their prayers for a Divine illumination, and that those prayers were not left unheard.

The study of classical literature has long occupied a large part of the education of Christian youth. It needs, of course, to be faithfully handled and wisely supplemented, but in the hands of truly Christian teachers it may become a distinct help to religious training. Let us not forget that the study of the Hortensius of Cicero was one of the first strong influences which stirred the heart of

St. Augustine to nobler aspirations. In Plato, in Seneca, in Epictetus, in Marcus Aurelius, we may often find the "*testimonium animæ naturaliter Christianæ.*" How can we better express the reality and blessing of Ethnic inspiration than in the sweet verses of the *Christian Year?*—

"And now another Canaan yields
   To Thine all-conquering Ark;
Fly from the 'old poetic' fields,
   Ye Paynim shadows dark!
Immortal Greece, dear land of glorious lays,
Lo! here the 'unknown God' of thy unconscious praise.

"The olive-wreath, the ivied wand,
   'The sword in myrtles drest,'
Each legend of the shadowy strand,
   Now wakes a vision blest;
As little children lisp, and tell of heaven,
So thoughts beyond their thought to those high bards were given."

ANCIENT EGYPTIAN SYSTEMS.

II.

By the Rev. GEORGE RAWLINSON, M.A., Canon of Canterbury Cathedral.

THE religious system of the ancient Egyptians, as we see it in the palmy days of Amenhotep II. and Thothmes III., or again in those of Seti I. and Rameses II., was, externally at any rate, a polytheism of a multitudinous and complicated character. In all the temples we see the kings worshipping a long string of gods and goddesses, each distinguished by a special name, a special form, and generally by special emblems. In the religious books, as the "Ritual of the Dead" and the "Book of Hades," there is the same multiplicity of deities, and the same apparent distinctness of each deity from all the rest. The myths present us with groups of gods, acting as a society or as a family, standing in diverse relations one towards another, each with his own personality, speaking to each other, giving or executing orders, offering counsel, sometimes quarrelling, or even fighting. The well-known Osirid myth associates together a group of seven divine personages:—Seb, Nut or Nutpe, Osiris, Isis, Set, Nephthys, and Horus, who play their several parts in the strange and weird drama. In the myth of the "Destruction of Mankind" there is another group of seven or eight :—Nun, Ra, Shu, Seb, Nut, Thoth, Tefnut, and (if she is distinct from Tefnut) Athor. When the Greeks began their attempts to systematise the Egyptian polytheism, they distinguished eight gods of the first rank, twelve of the second, and an indefinite number of the third. Moderns, who attempt to enumerate the "principal Egyptian deities," make them sixty-three or seventy-three, or some other large number. The Egyptians themselves spoke of "the *thousand* gods, the gods male, the gods female, those which are of the land of Egypt," and in this expression were probably far from intending to lay down a fixed limit.

When we examine, by the light of the ancient remains, the question whether this multiplicity of gods was an original element of the Egyptian religion or the result of growth and development, we seem to find reason for deciding in favour of the latter view. As we trace the religion backwards towards its source, the pantheon diminishes. Such deities as Anta or Anaïtis, Bar or Baal, Astaret or Ashtoreth, Reshpu or Reseph, and Ken or Kiun, were unknown in Egypt until the Semitic influx, which began about the twelfth dynasty. Ammon himself received no acknowledgment until the rise of Thebes to power a little earlier, neither did his contemplar deities, Maut and Khonsu. On an altar dedicated by Pepi, the third king of the sixth dynasty, which seems to be intended as a commemoration of all the gods, the number of the names does not exceed forty. Among these are such abstractions as "Seeing," "Hearing," "Year," "Age," "Eternity," "Life," "Stability," "Triumph," "Justification," which can scarcely have been regarded as real deities. If we deduct these, and some other equally doubtful entries, we may say that Pepi appears to have acknowledged about twenty-five deities. Following the stream of history somewhat farther up, we come to the pyramid period, for which the records are ample. These set before us as the objects of worship at the time about eighteen gods and goddesses:—Ra, Phthah, Khem, Kneph, Thoth, Neith, Seb, Nut, Osiris, Isis, Set, Horus, Anubis, Athor, Sokari, Ma, Saf, and Heka. Finally, in the pre-pyramid period we find but nine gods recognised:—Ra, Phthah, Osiris, Isis, Horus, Set, Anubis, Athor, and Sokari. These nine are perhaps reducible to seven, for the identity of Isis with Athor, and of Phthah with Sokari, is probable.

Thus Egyptian polytheism is seen to have been a gradual growth, and the question naturally arises, whether, if we could trace the stream a little farther back, a little nearer to its source, we should not find the multiplicity altogether disappear, and the polytheism shrink up into monotheism. As in Semitic theology El and Eliun, and Baal, and Marnas, and Adonai, and Moloch, and Ram or Rimmon, and Shaddai are originally only so many names for the one Supreme God, though later they became separate and grew into distinct personages, so it may be at any rate suspected that, in the Egyptian religion, the polytheism was to a large extent owing to the tyranny of language, the numerous *nomina* of the one God becoming by degrees distinct *numina*. One special cause of this in Egypt was the original separation and isolation of the different parts of the country, in which each nome was at first a distinct state with its own ruler, its own capital, its own worship, and its own name for the great object of worship, the god of its own temple. Ra was originally the one god of On (Heliopolis), Phthah of Memphis, Neith of Sais, Bast or Pasht of Bubastis, Sabak of Crocodilopolis, Osiris of Abydos, Mentu of Hermonthis, Ammon of Thebes,

Kneph or Num of Elephantine, Athor of Denderah. As Egypt became united, as the nomes were merged into kingdoms, the god-names obtained a wider acceptance, and so the pantheon grew. The kings, whose object it was to parade the wide extent of their dominion, gladly exhibited in their temple bas-reliefs, and in their tombs the long trains of local gods and goddesses, which showed that all the nomes were subject to their power; the priests, with a deeper mystic meaning, gladly employed the multitude of epithets at once to set forth the Divine nature and perfections, and to surround the higher truths of religion with a mysteriousness that should not be penetrable by the uninitiated.

We may trace three phases in the early Egyptian religion. First, there is a time when all worship is local—when at Memphis, and Sais, and Heliopolis, and Bubastis, and Pisebek, and Sesennu, and Abydos, and This, and Thebes, and Silsilis, and Elephantine, isolated worships, similar in general character, but differing in their symbolism and in the name under which they speak of the Supreme Being, prevail. Then follows a time in which sun-worship becomes general, not superseding the local cults, but being superadded to them. The Osirid myth is formed, and there comes to be throughout Egypt a recognition of the gods of the Osirid circle:

—Seb, Nut, Osiris, Isis, Nephthys, Set, Horus, in addition to the earlier local belief and cult, whatever it was. Finally, by the joint efforts of the kings and of the priests, an amalgamation is made of all the various local cults and names, a vast pantheon is created, which continually tends to grow, multiplicity is desired as implying richness, abstractions are made into deities, a special god is placed over each of the elements, over the seasons, and over every operation of Nature that can be conceived of as separate and distinct.

But the primitive monotheism, which this politico-hierarchic system concealed and overlaid, was never wholly suppressed. In the time of the fifth dynasty, long after the introduction of the Osirid circle of gods, we find simple monotheism expressed in the "Maxims of Ptah-hotep," with an artlessness and unconsciousness that clearly indicate a mind on which polytheism has taken no hold, which may have accepted it as a mode of representing deity to the vulgar mass, but has allowed it no place in the inward convictions of the religious consciousness. "Obedience," says Ptah-hotep, "is of God; disobedience is hateful to God;" and again, "Good for a man is the discipline of his father, of him from whom he has derived his being. It is a great satisfaction to obey his words;

for a good son is the gift of God;" and further, "If thou art known for thy wealth, and hast become a great lord, let not thy heart grow proud because of thy riches; for it is God who has given them unto thee." Later on, there is that curious mixture of monotheism with polytheism which has been called henotheism, a phase of religion under which the god who for the time is present to the worshipper's thought occupies and engrosses it so entirely as to become, as it were, the only god, and to be addressed with all the epithets suitable to the purest monotheism. Thus in one hymn Ammon is called "the Ancient of Heaven" (cf. Dan. vii. 9), "the Oldest of the Earth, Lord of all Existences, the Support of all Things, the One in his Works, Single among the Gods, Lord of Truth, Maker of Men, Creator of Things below and above, Enlightener of the Earth, Lord of Eternity, Maker Everlasting, Lord of Adoration and of Life, the One Maker of Existences." In another, Osiris is "the Eldest, the King of the Gods, the Feeder of Beings, the Ruler of the two Worlds, the Beneficent Spirit, Great in Dignity, Permanent in Empire." In a third, even so local and inconsiderable a deity as Hapi, the Nile-god, elsewhere spoken of as created by Osiris, becomes to his worshipper the sole representation of deity, and is addressed as

"Bringer of Food, Great Lord of Provisions, Creator of all Good Things, Lord of Terrors and of Choicest Joys, Giver of Life to all." It is said of him that "he is not graven in marble; he is not beheld; he is not adored in sanctuaries; his abode is not known; no shrine is found of his with painted figures; there is no building that can contain him; he hath no counsellor;" and again, "Unknown is his name in heaven; he doth not manifest his forms; vain are all representations."

The educated classes among the Egyptians went beyond henotheism. As Wilkinson long ago observed—"The priests who were initiated into, and who understood the mysteries of their religion, believed in one Deity alone, and in performing their adorations to any particular member of the pantheon, addressed themselves directly to the sole Ruler of the universe through that particular form. Each form (whether called Ptah, Amon, or any other of the figures representing various characters of the Deity) was one of His attributes; in the same manner as our expressions, 'the Creator,' 'the Omniscient,' 'the Almighty,' or any other title, indicate one and the same being." Similarly Lenormant:—"Au fond de la religion de ceux qui avaient approfondi la science religieuse se retrouvait la grande idée de l'unité de Dieu." The manifold gods of the popular mythology were understood by the educated to be either personified attributes of the Deity, or parts of the nature which He had created, considered as informed and inspired by Him. Num or Kneph represented the creative mind; Phthah, the creative hand, or act of creating; Maut represented matter; Ra, the sun; Khonsu, the moon; Seb, the earth; Khem, the generative power in Nature; Nut, the upper hemisphere of heaven; Athor, the lower world or under hemisphere; Thoth personified the Divine wisdom; Ammon, perhaps the Divine mysteriousness or incomprehensibility; Osiris (according to some), the Divine goodness. When an educated Egyptian worshipped Khem, or Kneph, or Ra, or Maut, or Osiris, or Thoth, or Ammon, he understood that he was worshipping the one God under some one of His forms, or in some one of His aspects. In this sense it is quite true to say, as Mr. Goodwin does, that "the recognition of one sole Creator and Governor of the earth and all its inhabitants was quite familiar to the Egyptians."

So far, then, as the primary truth of religion—the unity of God—is concerned, the relation borne by the Egyptian system or systems to Biblical theology is this—While the Bible proclaims, clearly and unmistakably, with a voice like that of a trumpet, the great fact that there is one and one only God, the Maker and Governor of the universe, the sole proper object of worship to men and angels, in ancient Egypt this truth was secretly inculcated by the priests, formed a part of the esoteric religion, was known to the initiated, while to the great mass of the people it was so veiled and overshadowed by a multitudinous polytheism, everywhere meeting the eye and the ear, as practically to be unknown, unrecognised, not even conceived of. The obscuration of the truth was brought about gradually. A primitive monotheism, derived from the primeval revelation made to mankind, was by degrees overlaid and hidden under a cloud of invented deities, originally attributes or manifestations of the one Supreme Being, but rapidly tending to detach themselves, and to become separate personalities. " L'idée de Dieu," as Lenormant says, " se confondit peu à peu avec les manifestations de sa puissance, ses attributs et ses qualités furent personifiés une foule d'agents secondaires, distribués dans un ordre hiérarchique, concourant à l'organisation générale du monde, et à la conservation des êtres. C'est ainsi que se forme ce polythéisme qui, dans la variété et la bizarrerie de ses symboles, finit par embrasser la nature entière."

If we compare the Egyptian idea of the nature

and attributes of the one God with that which is set before us in the theology of the Bible, we shall probably at first sight be surprised at the amount of resemblance. The Supreme God of the Egyptians is an Eternal Spirit, "the sole Producer of all things both in heaven and earth, Himself not produced of any," "the only true living God, self-originated," "who exists from the beginning," "who has made all things, but has not Himself been made." He is called "the Creator of Existences," "the Support of all Things," "the Lord of Eternity, of Life, of Wisdom;" and again, "the Lord of Terror," "He whose eye subdues the wicked." An inscrutable mystery attaches to Him. "His abode is not known;" "there is no building that can contain Him" (cf. 1 Kings viii. 27; Isa. lxvi. 1); "His name is hidden"—"unknown" even "in heaven;" His form is inconceivable—"He does not manifest it;" "vain are all representations." And He is omniscient. He is "the Lord of Wisdom whose precepts are wise"—"no one has ever been His counsellor" (cf. Isa. xl. 12–14); "He lies awake when all men sleep" (*ib.* 28); "He sees" and "knows all things." His moral character is in many respects beautifully drawn by the religious poets. He is "the Good God"—"beneficent in will and word;" "the Giver of all

Good Things" (cf. James i. 17); "the Lord of Mercy, most loving;" "the Hearer of Prayer"—"He fulfils the desires of them who cry to Him" (cf. Psalm cxlv. 19); "He listens to the poor in distress, and is gentle of heart when one cries to Him" (cf. 2 Cor. x. 1); "He giveth help;" He is "a Strong Defender"—"no help comes from any one except from Him;" "vainly do men trust to princes in their troubles" (cf. Psalm cxviii. 8, 9; cxlvi. 3). At the same time that He is so merciful, He is "the Lord of Truth;" "the Doer of Justice;" "He who maintains justice in the two worlds;" "He who overthrows and consumes His enemies." The only marked deficiency in the moral character of the Supreme God of the Egyptians which strikes the student of Egyptian texts, is the want of any insistence on His absolute purity and holiness, and a consequent toning down of that extreme awfulness which in the Biblical theology attaches to the Almighty. We miss parallel expressions to that of Isaiah (chap. lvii. 15)—"Thus saith the high and lofty One that inhabiteth eternity, whose name is Holy; I dwell in the high and holy place;" or that of Habakkuk (chap. i. 13)—"Thou art of purer eyes than to behold evil, and canst not look on iniquity;" or that of Bildad the Shuhite—

"The stars are not pure in Thy sight;" and again we miss parallel statements to those of the author of the Epistle to the Hebrews—"It is a fearful thing to fall into the hands of the living God" (chap. x. 31), and, "our God is a consuming fire" (chap. xii. 29).

We must further note that the religious elevation, whereof we have given specimens, is never long sustained in the Egyptian texts. There is nothing in any of the Sacred Books that can compare with the lofty flights of Isaiah or the magnificent descriptions of Job, or even with the deep devotion and spiritual elevation of the Psalms. Passing from Scripture to the Egyptian texts, we breathe a different atmosphere, we descend to a lower level. In the same hymn in which Amen, representing the Supreme God, has all the highest titles of divinity showered upon him, he is also given epithets which startle and shock the devout mind; *e.g.*, he is "the beautiful bull," "the bull of his mother in his field," "the good being *begotten of Phthah;*" "the gods *love his fragrance* when he comes from Arabia;" he is "a beautiful youth;" he has "strong, beautiful horns;" he "proceeds from the firmament," and is described unmistakably as the actual sun which rises and traverses the heavens and sets. He "rises in the eastern horizon, and sets in the western;" he "dawns on his children daily;" he is "lord of the boat and of the barge that conduct him through the firmament in peace;" he "sails in the heaven in tranquillity." Much as we would desire to give these expressions a mystic or symbolic meaning, they seem incapable of it; they constrain us to see in the great Amen nothing after all but a sun-god, an intelligence seated in the solar orb, circling round the earth day after day; a slave chained to the oar, with an existence which is one long monotony. How different from this is the Biblical conception of the Great Spirit, of whom heaven and earth, the sun and moon and stars, are mere creatures, set to perform their several tasks, "servants of His, that do His pleasure"!

Again, it cannot reasonably be denied that the Egyptian religion must have grievously lowered and debased the conception of the Divine nature in the minds of those who accepted it by its animal worship. It is an unworthy attempt on the part of a learned Egyptologist to throw dust in the eyes of the unlearned and ignorant, to assure them, as Mr. Goodwin does, that "probably the well-instructed Egyptians no more worshipped as gods crocodiles, ibises, and cats, than the Dutch do storks, or than we do the animals in the Zoological

Gardens." The Dutch do not put men to death for killing storks, as the Egyptians did those who killed hawks, or cats, or ibises. They would not, in case of a fire in one of their cities, leave the flames to spread as chance might direct, and concentrate all their attention and their efforts on preventing the storks from singeing their wings, as Herodotus tells us the Egyptians concentrated theirs on saving the cats. We keep our *foreign* animals in the Zoological Gardens as curiosities, that we may see what they are like. We do not lodge them in magnificent abodes, or have them attended by trains of priests, or lead them in procession through the streets for people to fall down before them and worship them, or proclaim a public festival when a new one makes his appearance in our midst, or go, one and all of us, into mourning on their decease, or spend twenty or thirty thousand pounds upon their funerals, as the Egyptians did with their Apis and Mnevis bulls at Memphis and Heliopolis. The fact is, that, according to all the ancient authorities, and according to the Egyptian remains themselves, the Apis and Mnevis bulls at Memphis and Heliopolis, and other sacred animals elsewhere, held the actual position of gods in Egypt, were called gods, were actually worshipped, had their own priests and temples, and were viewed as incarnations of deity. The ordinary inscription on the tomb of an Apis bull runs as follows:—" The —th year, the —th of the month —, under the sanctity of the Horus who makes strong the heart, the King of Upper and Lower Egypt, the Lord of the Northern and Southern regions, the Lord of Strength, the Ruler of the two Worlds, the Horus of gold, the Sun who rejoices the heart, the son of the Sun, —— (name of king), beloved of Api-Osiris, *the god* was embarked to unite himself with the good Amenti, and was given his reunion and his seat in the Kherneter, on the side of the west, at Phthah-Ka. The manifestation of *the sanctity of the God* towards heaven took place in the —th year, the —th of the month—; his birth took place in the —th year, on the —th of the month —, under the sanctity of the Horus who glorifies the heart, the Sun, the son of the Sun, —— (name of king), living for ever. His installation in the temple of Phthah took place in the —th year, on the —th of the month —, under the sanctity of the Horus who benefits the heart, the Sun who bestows goodness upon the heart, the son of the Sun, —— (name of king). The happy duration of *this god* was — years, — months, and — days. The good god, —— (name of king), arranged for *the august god* all the grave-clothes and other worked things, and all the ceremonies. This he did that he might obtain the gift of an eternal and powerful existence." It will be seen that the Apis bull is called a god four times over in his epitaph.

No doubt the bulk of the sacred animals were of less account, and were rather reverenced than worshipped. Still it was a religious feeling to which they appealed, not a sentiment of kindness merely, far less a feeling of curiosity. They were considered in a certain sense Divine, and the regard in which they were held could not but have absorbed an appreciable portion of the religious sentiment of the nation. Still it did, comparatively speaking, little harm. The animal-worship which was debasing and degrading, which lowered men's conceptions of the Divine nature, and was justly ridiculed by the Greeks, the Persians, and the Romans, was that of the Apis and Mnevis bulls, and of the other animals supposed to be gods incarnate.

The Egyptian animal-worship is thought by some to be a remnant of "totemism," a partial survival from the time when the nation consisted of a set of tribes, each of which regarded itself as descended from some animal or other. But this theory in no way rises above the dignity of an improbable conjecture. It was not their ancestors whom the

Egyptians connected with animal forms, but their gods; and from the gods they held that no human being was really descended (Herod. ii. 143). The true origin of the worship of animals in Egypt is probably to be found in that exaggerated symbolism which is characteristic of the Egyptian religion. Some resemblance, real or fancied, was traced, or thought to be traced, between the idiosyncrasy of some animal and the peculiar features of some god. Forthwith the animal became the symbol of the god, as the wise ibis of Thoth, the far-seeing hawk of Ra, the watchful dog of Anubis, the cow of bounteous Athor, the crocodile of awful Sabak, the hippopotamus of Taourt, the lion of Pasht or Sekhet. After this the deities were themselves represented in the form or with the head of the animal thus associated with them. Finally, the animals themselves, through this association, became sacred.

Biblical theology, it is evident, bears no relation at all to this element of the Egyptian religion, which is an excrescence or accretion, the result of human thought and fancy exercising itself in the domain of religion with too much freedom, and too little sense of the necessity of self-restraint.

ANCIENT EGYPTIAN SYSTEMS—
(Continued).

III.

By the Rev. GEORGE RAWLINSON, M.A., Canon of Canterbury Cathedral.

THE religious system of the ancient Egyptians is differentiated from all other non-Christian systems *most pointedly* in the stress that it laid upon the after life, and the detail into which it entered with respect to the conditions, trials, circumstances, and ultimate fate of the dead. It was the universal belief in Egypt, from a date long anterior to Abraham, that immediately after death the soul descended into the lower world (Amenti), and was conducted into the Hall of Truth, or "of the Two Truths," where it was judged in the presence of Osiris, and of his forty-two assessors, the "Lords of Truth" and judges of the dead. Anubis (Anepu), the "Director of the Weight," son of Osiris and Nephthys, brought forth a pair of scales, and, after placing in one of the scales a figure or emblem of Ma (Truth), set in the other a vase containing the good deeds of the deceased, Thoth—the Divine Wisdom—standing by the while with a tablet in his hand, whereon to record the result. If the good deeds preponderated, if they weighed down the scale wherein they were placed, then the happy soul was permitted to enter "the boat of the sun," and was conducted by good spirits to the Elysian fields (Aahlu), to the "Pools of Peace" and the dwelling-places of the blest. If, on the contrary, the good deeds were insufficient, if the scale containing them remained suspended in the air, then the unhappy soul was sentenced, according to the degree of its ill-desert, to begin a round of transmigrations in the bodies of more or less unclean animals; the number, nature, and duration of the transmigrations depending on the degree of the deceased's demerits, and the consequent length and severity of the punishment which he deserved or the purification which he needed. Ultimately, if after many trials sufficient purity was not attained, the wicked soul, which had proved itself incurable, underwent a final sentence at the hands of Osiris, Judge of the Dead, and being condemned to complete and absolute annihilation, was destroyed upon the steps of heaven by Shu, the Lord of Light. The good soul, having made a long peregrination through the infernal regions, encountering many dangers, and having then been freed from its infirmities by passing through the basin of purgatorial fire, guarded by the four ape-faced genii, was made the companion of Osiris for a period of three thousand years, after which it returned from Amenti, re-entered its former body, rose from the dead, and lived once more a human life on earth. This process was gone through again and again, until a certain mystic cycle of years became complete, when, to crown all, the good and blessed attained the final joy of union with God, being absorbed into the Divine essence from which they had once emanated, and so attaining the full perfection and true end of their existence.

A later form of the belief regarded each justified soul as in some sense absorbed into Osiris immediately upon its justification, and hence the name of Osiris was freely bestowed on each such soul. Individuality was not, however, wholly lost. The justified soul still bears its own earthly name, together with that of Osiris, and is conceived of as standing in a certain relation to its mummified body, which it occasionally revisits, and in the offerings made to which it participates. The clearness, definiteness, and precision of the Egyptian belief in respect of the future state is certainly in striking contrast to the dimness and indefiniteness in which the subject is left by the Biblical writers, especially those of the more early times. Mosaism pointedly avoided the entire subject of a future life, concentrating itself upon the duties of this life, and setting before men temporal rewards and punishments, with the object of keeping them within the line of their duties. As Moses cannot but have been thoroughly conversant with the Egyptian views with respect to a future existence and a judgment of all men after death according to their works, it is impossible to doubt that his reticence was intentional, premeditated, perhaps commanded. The fact was, that the Egyptian system, whatever amount of truth it contained—and we are far from denying that the amount was considerable—rested on no sound basis, was a fabric built up by fancy out of very questionable materials, and involved much false teaching of a practically dangerous character, against which Moses had to guard his countrymen.

I. The doctrine of absorption into the Divine essence, whether at death or ultimately, was a pantheistic conception, which involved logically the whole degrading theory of Pantheism. If the human spirit was to become at some future time a part of the Divine essence, then it must have been derived from that essence, not in the way of creation, but of emanation, and so must be really, during the whole period of its seemingly separate existence, a part of God. This doctrine leads to the most intolerable spiritual pride, the most ruinous self-conceit, the putting away of self-control as unnecessary, and belief in the indifferency of actions. If in Egypt it did not have these worst results, we must account for it by the fact that the Egyptian teaching on the subject was not uniform nor consistent; the defunct Egyptian of the time of Moses was at once Osiris, and not altogether Osiris; he "dwelt in the eternal seat"—he was the "triumphant one"—he had "splendour in heaven and power on earth;" yet he "went in and came out from his tomb;" he enjoyed the sepulchral meals that were offered to him by his relatives; he liked to feel the north wind blowing on him, and he refreshed himself beneath the branches of the trees which he had planted. As for the final absorption into God at the end of the mystic cycle of years, it was too remote an event to occupy the minds of living men, and probably only a few philosophers among the priests ever thought out its logical consequences.

II. The features of the future life, as set before the mass of the Egyptians by the priests, were not of such a character as to attract the approval of a divinely-inspired teacher like Moses. The *kas*, or spirits of the dead, were represented as "wandering over the earth, going to the tomb, visiting those who belonged to them, enjoying the offerings of their relations, and then disappearing to the body in the grave." Even in the "Fields of Peace," where they dwelt in Amenti, they prayed that some "might *come to them with jugs of beer and cakes,* the cakes of the lords of eternity," and hoped to "*receive slices from the joint upon the table of the great god.*" The most spiritual of their enjoyments were "the breathing of the delightful breezes of the north wind, the eating of bread, the gathering of flowers, and the receiving of food in felicity from the produce of the Sekhet Aahlu."

III. The Egyptian "justification" was not of such a nature that a Divine legislator could give it his sanction. An Egyptian, at the judgment, was supposed to appear before the assessors of Osiris, and to deny wholly that he had ever committed any of the forty-two sins of the Egyptian sacred code. "I have not blasphemed," he had to say; "I have not deceived; I have not stolen; I have not slain any one treacherously; I have not been cruel to any one; I have not caused disturbance; I have not been idle; I have not been drunken; I have not issued unjust orders; I have not been indiscreetly curious; I have not multiplied words in speaking; I have struck no one; I have caused fear to no one; I have slandered no one; I have not eaten my heart through envy; I have not reviled the face of the king nor the face of my father; I have not made false accusations; I have not kept milk from the mouth of sucklings; I have not caused abortion; I have not ill-used my slaves; I have not killed sacred beasts; I have not defiled the river; I have not polluted myself carnally; I have not taken the clothes of the dead," &c. He was to protest perfect sinlessness: "My mouth and my hands are pure," he was to say. As he quitted the Hall of the Two Truths, he was to repeat five times over the words, "I am pure." Thus he was to be justified by his own merits. He was not to throw himself on the Divine mercy, and confess himself "Unclean, unclean;" on the contrary, he was to claim that his actions had deserved an eternal reward.

IV. The original doctrine of retribution, of rewards and punishments distributed after death according to desert, was early corrupted and overlaid in the Egyptian system by an elaborate "Ritual of the Dead," which substituted, as the means of salvation, for inherent righteousness, a knowledge of certain elaborate prayers and set incantations, by the help of which alone could justified souls secure their passage from the Hall of the Two Truths, where they had been judged, to the "Pools of Peace," the blessed fields of Aahlu. Numerous and terrible perils lay in the way. Here crocodiles and lions, there vipers and serpents of huge size, in places monsters of indescribable form and of extreme ferocity, barred the way to the soul's farther progress, and had to be propitiated before they would allow the soul to pass onward. The propitiation was by means of charms or of set forms of prayer, which must be recited by the soul arrested on its course, each at the proper time and in the proper place. With a view to help the memory, if it failed, the most important passages of the ritual were inscribed in the inner part of the coffin wherein the mummy lay, or on the bandages wherewith it was swathed from head to foot, or upon the inner walls of the tomb. Sometimes even a complete copy of the book was buried with the corpse, in order that the *ka*, or soul, might refer to it for the proper prayer, charm, or invocation, whereby alone could the difficulties be surmounted which met the soul at every stage of its perilous journey. The effect of all this was to substitute a material for a moral righteousness—to make ultimate salvation depend on memory, acquaintance with formulæ, or ready access by priestly favour to the formulæ needed.

V. Moreover, the whole Egyptian belief on the subject of the dead was so inseparably bound up with the prevalent polytheism, worship of ancestors, and sun-worship, that a prudent legislator, having to legislate for a people of material tendencies, greatly inclined to idolatry, might well hesitate to lend any countenance to views in which the false and the true, the elevating and the degrading, were inseparably intermixed, and might be wise in determining to leave the future life in the vagueness and the mystery from which the daring speculations of the Egyptian priests had withdrawn it, and to concentrate men's attention on that present life which is their immediate concern, and the rightful conduct of which is the best preparation for whatever existence God designs them to lead in the world to come. The Egyptian priests, taking as their basis man's instinctive belief in his immortality, and his conviction that goodness must somewhere receive adequate reward, and wickedness adequate punishment, built up an artificial system of which much was purely fanciful, a large portion absolutely false, and only a comparatively small residuum sound and true. Biblical theology kept itself aloof from this mixed, fanciful system. It implied from the first, without distinctly teaching it, a life beyond the grave; it gradually brought this life more and more into prominence; by the time of Daniel (Dan. xii. 2) it hinted at immortality, and at a judgment; finally, by the mouth of Jesus, and of His "beloved disciple," it declared without ambiguity the nature of the judgment (Matt. xxv. 31–46; Rev. xx. 11–15), and the fate, respectively, of those who shall be condemned and of those who shall be acquitted. It left much still in obscurity, especially abstaining from any description of the life which the blessed lead in the other world. It thus avoids the almost inconceivable bathos of the Egyptian teaching, which told of "cakes" and "jugs of beer," and "slices from the joint which lay upon the table of the supreme god."

As the Egyptian religion was at once remarkably in advance of others, and at the same time in certain respects curiously mistaken and defective in its teachings on the subject of man's future destiny, so it was at once in advance of other systems and strangely defective on certain points in its teachings with respect to morality. The Egyptian idea of morality was predominantly negative. Justification was claimed, in the main, upon a series of negative declarations—"I have not blasphemed; I have not deceived," and the like. Hence the pleading of the soul newly arrived in Amenti before Osiris and his forty-two assessors has received the name of "the negative confession." But "the negative confession," extensive as it may appear to be, since it is a declaration of freedom from forty-two main sins, contains important omissions. One form alone of impurity is denied, and the omission of all others painfully reminds us of the charges brought against the Egyptians by the classical writers, who tax them both with religious impurity, and with a general laxity in the matter of the sexual relations. The charge is borne out by the levity of treatment which sexual irregularities receive at the hands of the native romance-writers, with whom, they are a stock subject, and from whom they get no word of blame. The state of morals thus indicated was a natural consequence of the impure rites which formed a part of the religion, and of the free toleration by the priest class of the extensive polygamy and the incest which were practised by the kings. Again, the cruel treatment *of enemies* was not disclaimed in the "negative confession;" and it is clear that it was widely and openly practised. Captives taken in war were either put to death by their captors, or carried off into a servitude of the most oppressive kind, involving in many cases continuous forced labour under the lash, and treatment such as made Egypt a "furnace of affliction" to the people of Israel. Another vice which the Egyptian was not required to disclaim, and which consequently flourished in the greatest luxuriance, was pride and self-conceit. The ordinary Egyptian was accustomed to declare himself, not merely before the assessors in Amenti, but on earth among his contemporaries, exempt from all human imperfection. "I was not an idler," says one; "I was no listener to the counsels of sloth; my name was not heard in the place of reproof. . . . . All men respected me. I gave water to the thirsty; I set the wanderer in his path; I took away the oppressor, and put a stop to violence." "I myself was just and true," writes another on his tombstone; "I was without malice, having put God in my heart, and being quick to discern His will. I have done good upon earth; I have harboured no prejudice; I have not been wicked; I have not approved of any offence or iniquity; I have taken pleasure in speaking the truth. . . . *Pure is my soul;* while living I bore no malice; *there are no errors attributable to me; no sins of mine are before the judges*. The men of the future, while they live, will be charmed by my remarkable merits." " I have come to thee," says another, " Lord of Tasert, Osiris, Prince of Abydos. I was law-abiding while upon earth; I did that which was right; I was *free from faults*." Here, however, as in so many other cases, the Egyptian system was not wholly consistent with itself. While the tone of self-glorification is *almost* universal, and king after king, noble after noble, courtier after courtier, calls on us from the tomb to admire his "remarkable merits," occasionally, but very rarely, there strikes upon the ear an undertone of self-humiliation and sadness, which affords a welcome relief. Conviction of sin has come home to a guilty soul, and the trembling heart pours itself out in prayer. " Come to me, O thou Sun," says a spirit thus oppressed. " Horus of the Horizon, give me help; thou art he that giveth help; there is no help without thee. Come to me, Tum; hear me, thou great god! My heart goeth forth towards On; let my desires be fulfilled; let my heart rejoice, my inmost heart rejoice in gladness. Hear my vows, my humble supplications, every day; hear my adorations every night—my cries of terror—cries that issue from my mouth, that come forth from it one by one. O Horus of the Horizon, there is none other beside thee, Protector of Millions, Deliverer of Tens of Thousands, Defender of him who calls upon thee, Lord of On! *Reproach me not for my many sins.* I am young and weak of body; I am a man without a heart. Anxiety preys upon me, as an ox feeds upon grass. If I pass the night in sleep, and therein find refreshment, anxiety nevertheless returns to me ere the day is done."

The positive side of the Egyptian morality contains some striking parallels with the teaching of the Bible. Monsieur F. Chabas has well compared the following passages:—

> "I gave my bread to the hungry,
> And drink to him that was athirst;
> I clothed the naked with garments,
> I sheltered the wanderer."
> ("Ritual of the Dead," ch. cxxv. § 38.)

and—

> "I was an hungered, and ye gave me meat;
> I was thirsty, and ye gave me drink;
> I was a stranger, and ye took me in;
> (I was) naked, and ye clothed me."
> (Matt. xxv. 35, 36.)

But he has failed to notice that the moral teaching put forward in them is that of the Old Testament, no less than of the New, dating in Biblical theology from the time of Isaiah, if not even from that of

Job. If we turn to Job's protestation of his integrity (Job xxxi.), we find the following:—"If I have withheld the poor from their desire, or have caused the eyes of the widow to fail, or have eaten my morsel myself alone, and the fatherless hath not eaten thereof; if I have seen any perish for want of clothing, or any poor without covering, if his loins have not blessed me, and if he were not warmed with the fleece of my sheep . . . then let mine arm fall from my shoulder-blade, and mine arm be broken from the bone" (verses 16–22). In Isaiah the resemblance is still closer. The fast that God has chosen—that pleases Him—is this:—"To deal thy bread to the hungry, and that thou bring the poor that are cast out to thy house—when thou seest the naked, that thou cover him; and that thou hide not thyself from thine own flesh" (ch. lviii. 7). Elementary as is the teaching, it has a beautiful simplicity, which will never lose its charm, and a far-reaching application, which will always save it from being commonplace or trite.

Monsieur Chabas has also noticed the accord between Egyptian and Biblical morality with respect to the duties of children towards their parents, and to the special blessing attached to their observance. As the Decalogue requires children to honour and obey their parents, and promises them long life as the reward of their filial piety (Ex. xx. 7), so in the maxims of Ptah-hotep we find it laid down that "the son who accepts the words of his father will grow old in consequence" —or, as it is elsewhere expressed, "will enjoy an honoured senility." To curse or revile a father was, by the Mosaic code, punishable with death (Ex. xxi. 17); under the Egyptian it was a deadly sin, punished by exclusion from heaven. Fleshly fathers were entitled to chasten their children under both codes; while smiting father and mother was, under each, an unpardonable offence. "Good for a son is the discipline of his father," is the Egyptian saying; "He that loveth his son chasteneth him betimes," is the dictum of the Bible.

It is, perhaps, still more remarkable that among the Egyptian moral precepts is found one which is a near equivalent of the command of Christ— "Swear not at all" (Matt. v. 34). The Jews were strictly forbidden under the Mosaic Law to swear *falsely* (Lev. xix. 12), and the third commandment may be understood as intended to check the habitual interlarding of the conversation with oaths quite unsuitable to the occasion. But no Biblical moralist earlier than the son of Sirach distinctly interdicted all oaths (or all but judicial oaths, which we must suppose excepted) as irreverent. In

Egypt, however, as early as the twelfth century B.C., it was laid down as "a true and just precept of the good doctrine contained in the ancient texts," that men were not to "open their mouth in swearing."

But though advanced in some respects, the Egyptian positive morality cannot fairly be said to have been, altogether, of a very elevated character, much less "to have fallen short in nothing of the teachings of Christianity," as one of its panegyrists has asserted. The list of virtues was a short one, scarcely including more than piety, truthfulness, justice, temperance, kindness towards the poor and afflicted, and obedience to parents and rulers. There was nothing heroic about the Egyptian morality. It inculcated no severe self-denial, no stern control of the passions, no love of enemies, no turning of the cheek to the smiter, no patient endurance of injuries, no humility, no real purity, no complete resignation to the Divine will under all circumstances. It was a comparatively easy code to keep, and we cannot be surprised that so many Egyptians were fully satisfied that they had kept it. If a man had been a fairly good son, an orderly subject, deeply respectful, not to say servile, when brought into contact with the monarch, regular in bringing the expected offerings to the temples and to the ancestral tomb, not haughty in his demeanour, not cruel in his treatment of his dependents, not given to drunkenness or to profane swearing, and tolerably charitable to the poor and distressed, he would naturally feel quite satisfied with himself, and entitled to declare, in the words of one Egyptian on his tomb, " I was a good man before the king; I shielded the weak against the strong; I did all good things when the time came to do them; I was pious towards my father, and did the will of my mother; I was kind-hearted towards my brethren. When calamity befell the land, I made the children live, I established the houses; I did for them all such good things as a father doth for his sons"—or, in the words of another, " I have done the behests of men, and the will of the gods; I have given bread to the hungry and satisfied the indigent; I have followed the god in his temple; my mouth hath not spoken insolently against my superior officers; there hath been no haughtiness in my carriage, but I have walked measuredly; I have performed the law which the king approved; I have understood his commands, and watched in my place to execute his will; I have risen up for his worship every day; I have given my mind to his words without considering how he regarded me: I have observed uprightness and fairness; I have understood when to keep silence." The self-complacency which characterises the Egyptian epitaphs is the correlative and the natural consequence of the easygoing moral system from which the Egyptians generally derived their sense of the extent of their duties.

ANCIENT CANAANITE RELIGIONS.

IV.

By the Rev. Wm. WRIGHT, D.D., Secretary to the British and Foreign Bible Society, and Author of "The Empire of the Hittites," &c.

THE scientific grouping of ancient religions is largely due to recent philological research. When Bopp, in his Comparative Grammar, drew attention to the relationships of certain European languages to the idioms of Persia and India, it was concluded that the Greeks and Romans had no more invented their religions than they had invented their languages. Their gods, like their words, were reckoned as heritages of the past. As the geologist examines the strata of the earth, so the philologist examines the structure of languages. Fossil words, by the processes of comparative philology, live again in the light and the local colour of bygone ages, and not only reveal the secrets of their own youth, but are eloquent as to the origin and growth of the current thought and religion of their time. The current language of an age embodies the living thought of that age, and beneath the dead crust of the language is discovered the religious sentiment which once touched the imagination, and fired the heart and swayed the religious instinct of the people. Through the letter of the word the spirit is reached, and thus comparative mythology, or the science of religion, is a branch of philology.

Comparative grammar, in recent years, has demonstrated that the language of Phœnicia was the language of Canaan; indeed Canaan, or Lowlands, was the designation by which the Phœnicians knew their own country before the descriptive title was extended to the whole of Palestine. The people of Phœnicia and the people of Canaan were brothers, and their gods and religion, like their language, were common to both people. There were differences of dialect among the inhabitants of ancient Canaan, but the former inhabitants of the land, subdued by the invading Israelites, were, with perhaps the exception of the retreating Hittites, branches of the same Semitic stock, one in language and religion.

The Phœnicians were the great commercial and colonising people of antiquity. Their narrow foothold between the mountains and the main was the commercial centre of the world. The coast villages became mighty cities, the storehouses of Eastern and Western merchandise. The desert caravans bore the luxuries of the East to the gates of Tyre and Sidon, and the hardy Phœnician sailors, from the terraced homes of Lebanon, steered their white-winged ships through all known seas, distributing the products of civilisation among the Western barbarians. The Phœnicians, the predecessors of the Anglo-Saxon race, pushed out from the contracted homeland their surplus and enterprising population, and planted colonies on the lines of their commerce. The Phœnician in search of gain, or of a new home, did not leave his religion behind him. The colonists erected splendid temples in the lands of their adoption to the gods of Phœnicia, and even in distant Ireland Phœnician influence is traced in the Baal fires and in the ancient worship of the Baal of heaven.

As to the real character of Phœnician religion, we have scarcely any information from the Phœnicians themselves. Josephus informs us that every Phœnician city had its collection of registers and public documents. It is believed that the Phœnicians may have written on clay like the Assyrians, and yet, notwithstanding the enormous number of colonies planted by the Phœnicians, and the marvellous commercial enterprise and literary carefulness of the people, a few short inscriptions and some sculptures and gems are as yet their only records of themselves. Philo of Byblus, in the reign of Hadrian, gave to the world what purported to be a version of Sanchoniathon's history of Phœnicia and Egypt. Some quotations made from Philo's work by Porphyrius found their way into the writings of Eusebius. Philo's work has been looked upon by some as a forgery, but it is probable that he had access to original Phœnician documents, even if Sanchoniathon may have been as shadowy a historian as our own Ossian. The portions of the work that have come down to us are confused fragments, but they supply a few threads which, joined with others, furnish a clue to the religion of the people.

In the paucity of material for coming to a satisfactory conclusion as to the religion of Phœnicia, the newly discovered records of the buried cities of Babylonia and Assyria come to our aid.

According to tradition the Phœnicians came from near the Persian Gulf, and it now appears that they spoke the same language as that employed by Abraham in Ur of the Chaldees. The unearthed libraries of Assyria have enabled the comparative grammarian to prove that the languages of the Phœnicians, the Canaanites, the Moabites, the Hebrews, and the Assyrians are not only descended from the same stock, but are closely allied to each other as different dialects of the same language. According to Professor Sayce, "Assyrian turns out to be very closely related to Hebrew, as closely related, in fact, as two strongly marked English dialects are to one another. There is no other Semitic language (except, of course, Phœnician, which is practically the same as Hebrew) which is so closely allied to it."[1] The Canaanitish religion thus differing from the Assyrian only as one English dialect differs from another, we may look to the Assyrian for information as to the religion of Canaan.

While the first wave of Semitic migration was settling in the Palm land, on the east coast of the Mediterranean, the Semites who remained in Babylonia were gaining the ascendency over their Accadian predecessors. Semitic force prevailed over Accadian, but Accadian religion and culture triumphed over the Semites. The gods of the Accadians were taken over by the Assyrians, who semiticised the civilisation, the culture, and the religion of the early inhabitants of Babylonia whom they supplanted. The religion of Assyria

[1] *Assyria: Its Princes and People*, p. 11.

was Accadianism in Semitic moulds, and comparative philology demonstrates that the religion of Assyria in its main features became the religion of the Canaanites, whether inhabiting the land of Palestine, or colonising the islands and shores of the Mediterranean.

"The Semitic," says Professor Max Müller, "like the Aryan languages, possesses a number of names of the Deity in common, which must have existed before the Southern, or Arabic, the Northern, or Aramaic, the middle, or Hebrew, branches, became permanently separated, and which, therefore, allow us an insight into the religious conceptions of the once united Semitic race long before Jehovah was worshipped by Abraham, or Baal was invoked in Phœnicia, or EL in Babylon." [1]

The Accadian El, or Ilu, is perhaps the earliest name by which the Deity was known. The name appears in Babylonia in Bab-*El*. In Hebrew, Ha-*El*, Beth-*El*, El-Elyon, &c. In Phœnician we have *El*, son of the earth, and Philo connects the word with Elohîm. It is the Ilâh, or Allah, of the Arabic tongue.

The god Bel, or Baal, was worshipped in Babylonia, Assyria, Phœnicia, Moab, Philistia, Carthage, and throughout the Phœnician colonies, and the

---

[1] *Introduction to the Science of Languages*, p. 110.

name still clings to distant lands with which the Phœnicians traded.

The name of the one Accadian goddess, Istar, may be read on the Moabite monument of King Mesha, and among the inscriptions of the city of Zenobia. The Semites gave to the name the feminine form Ashtoreth, by which she was known among the Canaanites, and she became the Astarté of Askelon and Paphos, and the Aphrodite of the Greeks.

Other deities, such as Melech, or Moloch, Adonai, or Adonis, may also be traced in the common language of the different branches of the Semitic peoples. As the language and chief deities of Canaan were in close affinity to those of the other branches of the Semitic family, so the religion of Canaan resembled closely the rites practised by the other Semitic peoples.

The centre and chief object of Canaanitish worship was the Sun-god, Baal; and the Baal religion was based largely on the feelings of reverence or awe. The Accadians considered that every object or phenomenon in Nature possessed a spirit, and that these multitudinous spirits were either benevolent or malevolent. When the Semitic Babylonians took over the Acadian Pantheon they changed Anu, the supreme Sky-god, into Shamas, the Sun-god, and they endowed him with the qualities of active benevolence and active malevolence.

The Canaanites adored the Sun-god, Baal, as the chaser away of darkness and cold, and the giver of light and heat. He was "Baal," the dual-natured deity of life and fruitfulness. The Baal, the male principle of life and reproduction in Nature, was worshipped by the Canaanites in conjunction with Ashéra, the female principle of Nature. They looked upon the Baal as the god of Heaven, who made earth fertile and gladsome, and whose function was recognised in all the generative forces of Nature.

Baal, the active principle of Nature, was generally allied with Ashéra, the passive; but he was sometimes associated with Ashtoreth or Astarté, and Baal in the plural was associated with Ashtoreth in the plural, as in 1 Sam. vii. 4, where it is said, "The children of Israel did put away Baalim and Ashtaroth, and served the Lord only."

The confusion that has arisen by confounding Ashéra with Ashtoreth has been accounted for by Professor Robertson-Smith in the following manner :—

"The planet Venus was worshipped in Assyria as the chaste goddess Istar, when she appeared as the morning star, and as the impure Beltis when she was the evening star. These two goddesses, associated yet contrasted, seem to correspond respectively to the chaste Ashtoreth and the foul Ashéra, though the distinction between the rising and setting planet was not kept up, and the nobler deity came at length to be viewed as the goddess of the moon."

The Sun-god, Baal, was malevolent when in the heat of summer he exhausted the sap of life, burnt up the grass, drunk the rivers dry, and slew the people with miasma fever. As calamities were supposed to befall the Accadians through the instrumentality of the malevolent spirits, so the Canaanites believed that calamities befell them through the wrath of Baal. In every form of evil they recognised the displeasure of Baal. Hence it became necessary to appease the god; and as the Accadians used to offer human sacrifices to avert the wrath of the malevolent Zi, or spirits, so the Canaanites sacrificed their firstborn sons to appease the relentless deity. The fiery Sun-god demanded a sacrifice by fire. The offering must be a real sacrifice. He would have nothing but the best, the firstborn, the only son, and the offering had to be made willingly, and with signs of gladness. The children were burnt alive, the victims and the image of the god being garlanded with flowers, and the hideous ceremony was accompanied with music and other signs of joy. Prof. Sayce, speaking of this act of Canaanitish worship, which became common among the Canaanites, says, "It was no sign of savagery or brutality, but of profound self-sacrifice, which led the worshipper to give even more than his own life to the offended gods. It was, in fact, a true *auto da fé*, or act of faith; and so deeply rooted was the conviction of its necessity, that not only did the Israelites yield again and again to its fascination, despite the remonstrances of the prophets, but in far later times, when Carthage had been overthrown by the Romans, all the edicts of the conquerors, all the vigilance of the police, were unable to prevent the horrible sacrifices from secretly taking place."

Notwithstanding the stern warnings against this form of Canaanite idolatry (Lev. xviii. 21, and xx. 2–5) the Israelites sometimes joined in the abominable sacrifices. We find the Kings Ahaz (2 Kings xvi. 3) and Manasseh (2 Kings xxi. 6) causing "their children to pass through the fire" to Baal. Nor is this phrase a mere *euphemism* to avoid the mention of a barbarous rite, as some suppose, but expresses the idea which underlay the sacrifice. The children by passing through the fire were purified from earthly dross, and rendered fit to enjoy the favour of the god.

Movers has clearly established the fact that Moloch is only a special development of Baal in his destructive instead of in his life-giving mood. And it was to Moloch, as king, that human sacrifices were offered. This is abundantly clear from the language of the prophets (Jer. xxxii. 35), "They built the high places of Baal, which are in the valley of the sons of Hinnom, to cause their sons and their daughters to pass through the fire to Moloch." (See also Jer. vii. 31; xix. 5.) As Creutzer has pointed out, Moloch the king, and Baal the lord, are simply different names of the Sun-god, but in altered relations—Moloch is the Sun, who, in his course through the signs of Zodiæ, burns up his own children.

Another form of Canaanitish worship, connected with the dual-natured god, became a snare to the people of Israel. Baal, as the active male principle associated in worship with the unchaste Ashéra, became the patron of sensuality and licensed harlotry. We see an instance of this worship at Baal-Peor (Num. xxv.) Baal was represented on the idolatrous high places by stone obelisks, or upright columns, while Ashéra (translated groves in the Authorised Version) was represented by tree trunks, or upright wooden posts. It is believed that these symbols had not always been associated with the foul rites of Baal, but that they had been the memorials of the places where worshippers had once been in contact with God (Gen. xxviii. 18, 22). In process of time they became the symbols of Nature-worship, and as such fell under the condemnation of the prophets of Jehovah (Isa. xvii. 8; xxvii. 9; Micah v. 13-14).

As the firstborn sons were passed through the fire to Baal-Molech, so chaste virgins were devoted to wickedness in the name of religion. But it was not religion. It was only Ritual, unconnected with morality. In these unspeakable rites the Baal demanded the purest, the loveliest, and the most tenderly loved, and Canaanitish religion compelled its devotees to comply with the requests of the deity. Fathers and mothers, with heroic self-sacrifice devoted their young daughters to the remorseless god, believing that they were performing acts of boundless merit in the sight of heaven. So completely may ecclesiastic ritual be divorced from morality!

It is no wonder that this form of Canaanitish worship was so hateful in the sight of God's prophets, or that such condign punishment was meted out to the chosen people when "they forsook the

Lord, and served Baal and Ashtoreth" (Judges ii. 13; iii. 7). Their "fathers dwelt on the other side of the flood (river) in old time, even Terah, the father of Abraham, and the father of Nahor; and they served other gods" (Joshua xxiv. 2). What made Abraham and his seed to differ from the Semitic worshippers of other gods? The one true God had called them to be His people.

According to Max Müller, "the worship of Jehovah made the Jews a peculiar people, the people of Jehovah, separated by their God, though not by their language, from the people of Chemosh, and from the worshippers of Baal and Ashtoreth. It was their faith in Jehovah that changed the wandering tribes of Israel into a nation." [1]

Abraham heard the voice and followed the leading of Jehovah, and he became the father of the chosen people, who in Egypt, in the desert, among the Canaanites, and the other peoples of the world, remained witnesses to the one Living and True God. Phœnicia might barter her merchandise in all lands; Egypt might erect her mighty monuments; the Hittites might beat back the tides of invasion; Greece might instruct the world in culture and artistic beauty; Rome might teach the

[1] *Introduction to the Science of Religion*, p. 86.

nations law and order; but the descendants of that one man, called by Jehovah out of Ur of the Chaldees, preserved among the nations the knowledge of a personal holy God nigh at hand, who knoweth the righteous and who will "by no means clear the guilty."

How did it happen that the other Semitic peoples differed from the seed of Abraham by practising crime-stained religions? They too had heard the voice of "the one Living and True God." Canon Rawlinson, in his admirable tract on "The Early Prevalence of Monotheistic Beliefs," tells us "that in the early times, everywhere, or almost everywhere, belief in the unity of God existed." This is admitted generally, as regards the Semitic peoples, and it can be demonstrated from their inscriptions and their literature. What then is the secret of their religious degradation? The true scientific historical answer is given by the Apostle Paul: "Because that knowing God, they glorified Him not as God, neither gave thanks; but became vain in their reasonings, and their senseless heart was darkened. Professing themselves to be wise, they became fools, and changed the glory of the incorruptible God for the likeness of an image of corruptible man . . . wherefore God gave them up in the lusts of their hearts unto uncleanness, that their bodies should be dishonoured among themselves; for that they changed the truth of God for a lie, and worshipped and served the creature rather than the Creator, who is blessed for ever. Amen."

EARLIER HELLENIC RELIGIONS.

V.

By the Rev. EDWIN JOHNSON, M.A., late Professor of Classical Literature, New College, London.

NO one who has lived with the Greek religious traditions—the deposit of a dateless antiquity—long enough to appreciate their profound significance in the life of the people, and through them upon our own culture, can care to deal in hasty generalisations upon a subject so far-reaching in its scope as that which is stated at the head of this paper.

What can we do beyond rapidly indicating a few points of view, from which long perspectives profitable study open out? Such a standpoint, for example, is the period of Alexander and his successors, when the Greek language, Greek manners, Greek intuitions and philosophies made their way in Asia Minor, in Palestine, and, above all, in Alexandria. The Septuagint translation of the Hebrew Scriptures marks an epoch of the greatest moment in connection with the origins of our religion. The Greek myth of the miraculous unanimity of the translators[1] witnesses to this in one way. In another way, the feeling of Jewish doctors witnesses to the same thing. Denunciations of the sacrilegious act occur in the Talmud; for it was thought that a garbled version of the sacred records had been given to the world.[2] And hatred of swine and hatred of Greek learning seem to have been passions of equal strength.

Yet this is but one side of the case. A recoil was certain to follow from the first impetuous attack on a thing so all-pervading as Greek culture. And Dr Joel, the accomplished Rabbi of Breslau, has recently shown the other aspect of the matter. When the boy Ovid—as the tale runs—promised his father, after a beating, that he would give up verse making, he did so—in a hexameter! Similarly, the Rabbins rebuked the teaching of Greek, using Greek words in the act. Some of them even recommended Greek for girls. And the time came when proselytising Pharisees found the Septuagint useful, probably indispensable, in their work.[3] A stream takes colour from the bed through which it

---

[1] See Pseudo-Justin Martyr, *Cohort*, 13.
[2] Joel, *Blicke*. Edersheim, *Life of Jesus*, i. 30.
[3] Stapfer, *La Palestine au temps de Jesus Christ*.

flows; and that, from about two centuries before Christ, the oracles of the Hebrew prophets should have been conveyed to the world through the vehicle of the Greek *logos*, is one of the most important facts in the history of our religion. This wedding of Jewish substance with Hellenic form reaches its complete expression in Philo, a most epochal man.[1] Not without reason have scholars seen in him the father of Catholic theology, or the fount and origin of that mystical apprehension of the Old Testament Scriptures which has obtained ever since his day, and which will to all appearance still obtain. There seems no reason why Philo himself should not have embraced the new faith which was destined to spiritual empire: he was not a Judaiser, but rather a Helleniser; not a zealot for the observance of the Law, but rather a champion of spiritual freedom. He reads the current ideas of the educated world into the Hebrew Scriptures, not out of them.

But the name of Philo reminds us of his embassy to Rome, and of Apion, the slanderous Greek who went with him, and whom Josephus later so severely handled; and this again reminds us of the bitter feuds between Greeks and Jews

---

[1] Parallels between him and the recently discovered *Didaché* of the Apostles are shown in the edition of Massebieau.

at Alexandria, and the unhappy mutual aspersions in which they indulged. Here again is a point of moment in reference to our subject. In that intense and long rivalry of two conquered peoples,—both so highly endowed,—for spiritual mastery over their conquerors, which in the end prevailed, Jews or Hellenes? Is our religion more a debtor, humanly and historically speaking, to these or to those? Or are we to see in Christianity, after the same manner of speaking, a chemic combination of the Hellenic with the Hebrew spirit?[1] Surely these are questions for patient analytic study in detail, rather than for swift and sweeping decision. To say nothing of the strong contrast between such writings as the "Book of Enoch," and the writings of the Greek apologists and fathers, in the New Testament itself the diverse currents of theological belief, the Judaic and the anti-Judaic feeling, are too marked not to demand renewed inquiry on the part of every thoughtful student.

Let us select another standpoint. Let us plant ourselves in Hellas itself early in the second century A.D. Here we are in the hands of a guide

---

[1] On *Early Christianity, Rooted in the Old Testament and the Hellenic Spirit,*—Cf. Harnack on Havet's *Le Christianisme* in *Theol. Lit. Ztg.*, 1885.

and witness whom we cannot too highly value, Pausanias, an Asiatic Greek, a man of plain and unsophisticated thought, of competent learning, of simple piety, a man to be respected. After all that has been written on the subject, let us repeat what others have said before, that the *Periegesis* of this writer is our best introduction, on the whole, to the story of Greek religion and mythology. But this is a book you must pore over for years. The information Pausanias gives us is often far from self-intelligible. When our curiosity is excited by the hope of discovering something, our guide tells us that he is under the vow of an initiate, or that he is warned by a dream not to divulge the secret truth. Still, much may be gleaned by patient thought and comparison; and the sense grows upon us in this study that nowhere was religion held in a more intense and awe-stricken manner, nowhere was the popular intuition more ghostly, more saturated with the presence of spiritual life and activity than in ancient Hellas. Another book, dense with tragedies and horrors, is the *Bibliotheca* of Apollodoros.[1] No one who desires to get a deep impression of the religious ideas of the Greeks should omit the reading of the legends, as they here are

[1] c. 115 B.C.

evidently told without a touch of extenuation. A student will be pardoned if he insists that the subject cannot be "got up" from handbooks, nor yet from the perusal of Mr. Morris's "Epic of Hades." The most striking and luminous commentary on the Greek religious myths that has yet been furnished, is to be found in the lore of negroes and other tribes of the great continents, and of the islands of the present day. Things that are dark and enigmatic to us in the mythographers would be perfectly intelligible to the savage, if rendered into his tongue. The fear of the ghosts of the dead, who pass now under the name of "Heroes," now under that of "Dæmons," is the one pole of Greek religion; the other is the belief in gods who were saviours, atoners, purifiers, healers, imparters of dreams and of oracles.

If we desire to study the influence of Greek religious conceptions upon Christian theology, we can hardly do better than compare Pausanias with Justin Martyr, who is nearly his contemporary. There are points in this comparison which will strike every student coming freshly to the subject with great force. For example, the conception of incarnate, human, suffering, atoning deity is not once, but many times, exhibited in the Greek religious myths, in a manner certainly less refined than that of the Gospels, but one that indicates intense popular belief and pathos. The conception of the mother goddess, in some cases the union of the conceptions of maiden and mother (Athena, Artemis), was also mightily endeared to the Hellenes. We cannot wonder at the enthronement of the Panagia on the Athenian Acropolis in place of her who sprang from the brain of Zeus. Justin Martyr's "Apology" and "Dialogue with Trypho" show how keenly he felt the force of Hellenic analogies to Christianity.[1] But how does he dispose of them? In a way that can satisfy nowadays no common-sense Christian. The birth legends of the gods are set down to the invention of "wicked dæmons." The resemblance between the mysterious rites of the god Mithras and the Eucharist is ascribed to the like devilish imitation. But the worship of Mithras long antedates Christianity. How does Justin distinguish the Christian beliefs in the incarnation of the atoning cross from corresponding heathen beliefs? He finds them prefigured in the Old Testament. Hardly would an intelligent apologist of the present day care to use such arguments, or think that other than mischief could be done by them. But Justin's method is another

[1] *Apol.* I, 21, 54, 62, 64, 66; *Dial. c. Tryph.* 69, 70.

remarkable proof of the powerful spell exerted by the Hebrew Scriptures in the propagation of the new faith—interpreted, that is, and suffused by Greek reasonings. The strong thing in Justin Martyr is his doctrine of the immanence of the *logos* in Socrates, and in the "Barbarians."[1] Had he been consistent with that, he might have felt his way to the true basis of "Christian evidences," namely, that our religion has its foundation in the conscience, the affections, and the ideal nature of man. As they stand, his "apologies" awaken doubts which they cannot quell; and one cannot conceive of any but the weakest heads converted whether from Judaism or from paganism by them. The analogies of the supernatural in Hellenism and in Christianity, which his "wicked demons," *ex machina*, are introduced to explain, still demand our careful examination. Are they possibly, like other cases of reputed analogy, resolvable into identities of intuition? The demands of a true sacred science, a sacred anthropology, if you will, are not met till these and kindred problems are in all candour and earnestness grappled with.

Pausanias, living in the time of Hadrian and

[1] See the recent treatise of Professor V. G. Allen, *The Continuity of Christian Thought*.

the Antonines, apparently knows nothing of the new religious movement which was destined to dispossess gods and heroes from the shrines he visited with all a pilgrim's zeal. And his knowledge of the Jews is as limited as that of Plutarch, of Tacitus, and other writers of the first two centuries. Pausanias has heard of the Sabbath of the Jews, and of their prophetic lore. And there rises before his imagination the figure of "an oracular woman among the Hebrews beyond Palestine, whose name was Sabbé, and who was said to be daughter of Berosus and of Erymanthé. Some call her the Babylonian and others the Egyptian Sibyll" (10, 12, 5). Compare the idle tales about early Jewish history in Tacitus' "Histories" (v. 1 ff.) and in the "Epitome" of Junian Justin (c. 160 A.D.): what a gulf, caused by ignorance, deepened by antipathy, is fixed between the Roman and the Jewish and early Christian world! The genial and learned Plutarch (c. 100 A.D.) made the profound discovery that the "God of the Hebrews" was none other than Dionysos, apparently because at the Feast of Tabernacles wine was enjoyed, and an invocation was made which sounded like a name of the Greek god![1] A little later Tacitus (c. 116 A.D.) was writing down (the first time, probably, a

---

[1] *Symp.* iv. and foll.

Roman pen dropped the word) the *Christiani* and their "deadly superstition." During the second century, Greek and Roman religions, ever in spiritual alliance, the Egyptian rites of Isis and the Persian rites of Mithras still "held the field." How did Christianity attain to spiritual empire? How did it quell those "wicked demons"? By exorcism in the name of Jesus, is the chief explanation of Justin Martyr. As the Christian Church has long ceased to recognise the functions of the exorcist, this is for us hardly an intelligible explanation. Nor can we find what we need in that *naïve* literature which passes under the name of the "Apostolic Fathers!"[1] Massive popular movements and changes are never traceable to origins of that kind. In truth, the whole progress of Christianity from the time of Trajan and Hadrian, when it began to make itself seriously felt, is like the course of one of the subterranean rivers of Greece. We cannot adequately trace it in any written sources. It is sometimes said that heathendom "perished before the blows" of the Christian apologists and fathers. But it is difficult to think of anything being overcome by

[1] The first six chapters of the *Didaché* compared with *Ep. Barnabae* 18–20, and *Apost. Constt.*, bk. vii., also with *Testaments of the Twelve Patriarchs*, are richly ethical, *not* theological. See Dr. Warfield's art. in *Bibl. Sacra.*, Jan. 1886.

their declamations, for the most part so weak
and rhetorical. There were in the second and
the third century men far more than a match for
the "fathers" in point of learning and art, had
the future of Christianity depended on such re-
sources. It is painful in this respect to turn from
the pages of Plutarch, of Lucian, of Athenaeus, of
Pausanias, and again from Plotinus and Porphyry,
to the new polemists. It is an exchange of intellectual wealth for poverty. The life of the mass
of the people is little affected by controversies of
the educated. It is a still life; it goes on from
generation to generation, stirred with the like
pathos, nourished by the same thoughts, rooted
in the associations of the old festivals. Names
change, but the time-honoured customs are kept
up under them, until they are put down by force
or their profit ceases. A compromise was silently
going on during these times; the early Jewish-
Christian conception of the Christ, and the expectation of the Parousia, passed away; the demands
of a rigid monotheism yielded to the prevalence of
the Hellenic spirit, which finally triumphed at the
Council of Nicæa.

If, now, we take our stand with the fathers of
the third and fourth century, we find the whole
representation of Christian dogma coloured by old

Hellenic feeling and intuition. Take the dogma of the atonement. It is startling to modern ideas to find the sacrifice of Christ represented as a ransom paid to the devil on behalf of the human race, in consequence of a Divine pact.[1] Yet so Origen and Basil taught, with the use of imagery the most realistic and coarse. They did but fall in with prevailing conceptions. For what lay implicit in the legend of Apollo and his combat with the fiendish Python at Delphi, was the belief that the god, menaced at his birth by infernal power, was destined to overcome it, and that by self-sacrifice. While the heathen Plutarch expresses distaste for the tale of the god and the serpent told by the *theologoi* of Delphi, the Christian Minucius Felix, on the other hand, tells us that the tradition ran that the god was swallowed up of the Python. It may be inferred that the Christian atonement could not be understood by the people except under analogies borrowed from the old religions. And so with other matters. The old idea of initiation in the mysteries, and of a secret knowledge reserved for the few, is kept up in Chrysostom, who very frequently uses the phrase, "The initiated know."[2]

[1] See Mr. Oxenham's work on *The Atonement*, 2d ed.

[2] It is noteworthy also that this distinction of *mysts* and *amysts* is already in Philo.

If we study only the lore of leading Hellenic deities in historical times, Zeus, Apollo, Dionysos, we cannot but feel how fertile a bed had long been preparing for the new seed. That lore contains, under dramatic forms of narrative, representations the most tragic of the necessity of human sacrifice, of the slaying father and the slain son, the vicarious animal substitute, of the hereditary blood-guilt only to be wiped out by annual or other periodic atonements and purifications. The need of *willinghood* on the part of the human victims is also strongly impressed in many legends of a most thrilling character. The rites of Dionysos Eleutherios, the Liberator, have been well compared with the Paschal Feast, when the one sacrifice of the tribal god on behalf of his people, doing away with the cruel necessity of the slaughter of their own children, is thankfully commemorated.[1]

With regard to the future life, there is no reason to suppose that it was ever doubted of by the general mind in Greece. Initiation was craved because it was believed to ensure well-being both in the present life and in the life to come. It is a charge frequently brought by the early Christians against the heathen, that they worshipped " dead

[1] *Cf.* Julius Lippert, Die *Religg. der Europ. Cultur-Völker*, one of the most luminous of recent writers on these subjects.

gods." Certainly the ancestral tomb was the great focus of Hellenic piety. But the departed were the spiritually living in the belief of the people. And the idea of the baptism in fire by which the *humanum onus*, the burden of flesh and blood, might be removed and immortality be secured, survived and reasserted itself in the doctrine of purgatory.

Christian teachers came bringing a message of *sotéria*, of salvation to the world. But the mind of the heathen was no blank in respect to the nature of *sotéria*. He meant by it the aversion of disease from the body, famine from the fields, defence against the power of evil spirits, oracular guidance for the future, good hopes for all time. There was an intense craving for salvation in the Hellenic world, in this sense, at the beginning of our era, a deep and sorrowful sense of degradation from a once happier state. One of the most noteworthy passages in Pausanias is that where his mind reverts to blessed times when the gods held close communion with mortals, and were born from mortals. The great fame of the god Asklépios (Aesculapius) in Argolis and Athens during historical times is another striking evidence of the state of popular feeling. His worship was the centre of a great system of "faith-healing." The spring and the gymnasium lay hard by the temple. Pilgrims were believed to gain invigoration for the body and comfort for the mind in nightly visions. The god was held to have raised many heroes from the dead.

When we consider how sharply and sternly the most enlightened Jewish spirits, and again the Jewish-Christian "Apostles and prophets," of whose life and teaching so interesting glimpses are given us in the *Didaché*, opposed not only common heathen vices of the flesh, but also the practices of sorcery and divination, so rife in the Hellenic-Roman religions; how at the same time they met the yearning for salvation by the preaching of a creed at once sublime and simple, a morality in every sense sound and sweet: we may, perhaps, see where the victorious principle in the new religion was felt to lie. But as ever in human affairs, the tide rolled back; once more, *victi victoribus leges dederunt*. Heathendom reconquered most of its lost ground, even as Rome reconquered in Southern Europe after the Reformation. If the question be asked, "Is the religion of the mass of the people under the rule of the Greek and Roman Churches at the present day more heathen or Christian?" it must be answered that the whole question of the relations of new religions to old, partly antipathetic, partly sympathetic, demands ever fresh consideration. Beneath all historical changes, there ever remain some unchanging elements. To detect these is to get at the heart of the matter, for, ideally or spiritually speaking, there is but one religion. If, however, it be still, to every serious student, one of the most difficult things in the world to understand the history of our religion during the first two centuries, how much more so to understand those systems which had for so many centuries been preparing the ground for it in Greek and Roman culture. Among the many works we have consulted on the subject, we are inclined to think the work of Hartung on the Religion and Mythology of the Greeks will be found most suggestive to the general student. The mere examination of the rich religious vocabulary of the Greeks will of itself teach how mistaken it is to assume, as has been often done, that "Nature worship" rather than spiritual experience lies at the foundation of their religions.

THE JEWISH FAITH.

VI.

By Rabbi G. J. EMANUEL, B.A., of the Jews' Synagogue, Birmingham.

THERE are few more gratifying signs of our advanced and still advancing civilisation, than the marked and continually growing decrease of the animosity arising from difference of religious belief. In times past, men who, but for this difference, might have been friendly neighbours and mutually helpful fellow-citizens, were thereby separated into hostile bands. Dogmas rose up between them like huge walls; and from behind these walls, within which they stood like armed garrisons, they glared angrily out on all beyond the narrow boundaries of their sect. These walls have been lowered, the light of reason has entered the dark enclosures, the free air of liberty has swept through the close penfolds, and men, casting down their weapons, wonder why they regarded as enemies those who but exercised like themselves the godlike faculty of thought, and stood firm to their convictions.

A most striking and significant instance of this welcome change, is furnished by the changed relations of Judaism and Christianity. Christianity could once see in Judaism only blind, obstinate, wilful and sinful disbelief, an infatuated clinging to what it denounced as superstitious practices, a mad rejection of what it proclaimed the only possibility of salvation. While Judaism could see in Christianity only an active denial of its most cherished convictions—denial of God's Unity, denial of God's spirituality, denial of God's unswerving justice in rewarding the good and punishing the sinful—idolatry the more hopeless because bound up with it was belief in the true God—and withal, a ferocious enemy and implacable persecutor.

The two faiths are beginning to understand each other better. Christianity does Judaism the justice of admitting that it has moulded a race marked, if not by heroic, at least by substantial virtues—by parental care, conjugal fidelity, and filial affection; by brotherly love, tender compassion, large-hearted philanthropy, and a passionate attachment to liberty. While Judaism gladly acknowledges that "Christianity has carried the golden germs of religion and morality, long hidden in the schools of the learned, into the market of humanity, and has communicated that 'Kingdom of Heaven' of which the Talmud is full from the first page to the last, to the herd, to the lepers."[1]

We seek now not the differences, but the points of contact between the two religions, and we find them to be numerous and vital. And who will wonder at it who remembers that the New Testament was written, as Lightfoot puts it, "among Jews, by Jews, for Jews."

Lord Beaconsfield, in one of his earlier works, speaks of Christianity as the developed religion of the ancient Israelites, and of Judaism as that religion suddenly arrested in its growth and petrified. A truer description would be that Judaism and Christianity are alike evolutions differentiated from one common stock, that *stock* being the conceptions and practices held by the remarkable race that lived and ruled in Palestine from the time of Moses to the Common Era, a period of about 1400 years.

It is not for us here to discuss the origin of these conceptions and practices. On this point there will always be, as there always has been, two opinions wide apart as the poles. The critical student will seek their source in the religious system of the ancient Egyptians, in the travelled experience and

[1] Deutsch's *Literary Remains*, page 27.

ripe sagacity of Israel's leader, in the attempts to explain the phenomena of Nature and the ceremonies arising therefrom, which, following the same laws of thought, are so strikingly similar in early races of widely different types and locales. While the pious Jew and the devout Christian will be content with the all-sufficient explanation, that these conceptions and practices were divinely communicated to the inspired legislator of the Israelitish people.

Waiving then the question of their origin, let us seek to draw a faithful picture of those principles and institutions which formed the foundation alike of Christianity and modern Judaism.

First and foremost among these principles is the conception of the Deity, and of His relations to all besides Him.

The God of Israel is more than the God of gods, in the sense that He is greater than the deities worshipped by other nations; He is sole God, all others are idols, "with eyes that see not and ears that hear not"—*nothings*—powerless to help their most devoted worshippers. Self-Existent and Eternal (as exhibited in His name Jehovah, or Jahveh, from the Hebrew, "to be"), He is Creator of the universe and of man. But power is the least of His attributes. He is scrupulously just, infinitely good, tenderly merciful; patiently bearing sin, that the sinner may repent, but punishing the persistent sinner, and accepting no ransom except the ransom of remorse and return to right-doing. He is absolutely spiritual, free from corporeality and all its attendant defects. And He is One of a Unity rigorously severe, " Hear, O Israel! the Lord thy God, the Lord is One" (Deut. vi. 4).

It is worthy of note here, how the derived religions—modern Judaism and Christianity—while agreeing in adopting *en bloc* these ancient conceptions of the Deity, have diverged in the development of these principles, the former in the direction of severity, the latter in the direction of laxity.

The *Israelite* in Canaan was ever prone to make material representations of the Supreme—the *Jew* throughout the world will suffer no sculptured figure in his synagogue, nor even pictorial form, to disturb his profound sense of the spirituality of the Being he worships; but the Christian conceives the Deity as having been for years incarnated in a human creature.

The ancient Israelite, though his prophets hurled ridicule and invective against the notion, thought that the death of the animal he sacrificed expiated his sin and saved his life—the modern Jew, on the great Day of Atonement, proclaims that only prayer, good deeds, and repentance, can revoke the decree pronounced on the sinner; the Christian hopes and believes that the sufferings and death of Jesus atone his guilt and secure his salvation.

Finally, the Israelites of Palestine, despite the terrible penalties that instantly followed it, fell again and again under the fascination of idolatry. The watchword of Judaism at the present day is the Unity of God; the first words of prayer the Jewish child learns to utter, the last words of prayer that fall on the ears of the Jew at the moment of death, are the words already quoted: "Hear, O Israel! the Lord our God, the Lord is One;" while Christianity adores a holy trinity, God the Father, God the Son, God the Holy Ghost.

To resume—The God of Israel, the Creator of all, is the Father of all. All nations are His, and all are dear to Him. He took Israel as His chosen people, not in the sense that He would pet and favour them at the expense of other nations, or that He would permit them to indulge with impunity in vice and sin, but in the sense that He took them to do a great work, to perform a service on which He set great value, viz., that they should be " His kingdom of priests," teachers to the world of His truth and worship. Thus God's selection of Israel was an evidence of His universal love. Nor was man only the object of His affectionate regard—He looked with consideration on the lower productions of His creative power. True, He gave over all other living creatures to man for his use and benefit, but man was not to abuse his power. He might slaughter animals for food, but he was to inflict no unnecessary pain upon them; he might employ them in labour, but he might not overwork them, their burdens were not to be made too heavy, and they too were to rest on the holy Sabbath-day. Their *feelings*, so to speak, were to be respected: "Thou shalt not muzzle the ox when he treadeth out the corn" (Deut. xxv. 4). The dumb creature was not to be tantalised by the sight of the dainty on which he was working while he was prevented from taking a mouthful.

The God of Israel is pure and holy, and His people must become distinguished by the same qualities. They were to practise a morality which would do honour to the most advanced race of the nineteenth century, and which formed a marked contrast to the lawlessness and licentiousness prevalent alike among the Egyptians and Canaanites.

The relations between the sexes were to be characterised by refinement and mutual fidelity. All incestuous connections were to be avoided; the seducer was to marry his victim by a union that no divorce could dissolve (Deut. xxii. 29); adultery was to be purged by the death of the guilty ones (Deut. xxii. 22). And the purity acquired by a lofty morality was to be maintained by careful separation from all that could defile the body or disturb the mind; hence, probably, the laws concerning Levitical purity and dietary laws.

The relations between man and man were to be marked by strictest justice and tenderest love. Wrong should not be committed, either by act (sixth, seventh, and eighth commandments), or by word (ninth), or even by thought (tenth). And wrong inflicted should not be revenged, or even borne in mind (Lev. xix. 18).

Judaism and Christianity have alike inherited these noble conceptions of human relations, but Judaism has emphasised justice as the fundamental virtue, while Christianity identifies itself with love. The modern Jewish term for philanthropy, almsgiving, is צְדָקָה "justice," "righteousness," while the virtue constantly joined to the adjective Christian is charity—"Christian charity." But "Thou shalt love thy neighbour as thyself" (Lev. xix. 18) is still a precept acknowledged and largely obeyed by Jews as well as Christians.

The God of Israel, Creator and Sustainer, in every way the Benefactor of His people, was to be regarded by them with reverence and affection, was to be obeyed and worshipped. Days were to be observed holy to Him—the Sabbath, as their testimony to His mighty and beneficent work in creation; the Festivals and the Sabbath, too, as their testimony to His mighty and beneficent work in the deliverance from Egypt, the giving of the Law, the protection of His people in the wilderness, and in presenting, year by year, His gracious gift of the earth's products. Worship was to be manifested mainly in the one form known to the ancient world, the presentation of offerings. But it is to be noted that sacrifices for sins to God were to be preceded by confession (Lev. xvi. 21), for sins to man by restitution (Lev. v. 23); thank-offerings were to be accompanied by a declaration of God's goodness and of the gratitude of the worshipper (Deut. xxvi. 1-11), while the whole institution of sacrifices is introduced in such a way as represents it rather as regulating an existing practice than as establishing it as God's chosen form of service (Lev. i. 2). Thus the prophet Jeremiah (vii. 22) says: "For I spake not unto your fathers nor commanded them in the day that I brought them out of the land of Egypt concerning burnt-offerings and sacrifices." And all the prophets and psalmists speak of them as being of little value in God's eyes.

One further element of the ancient religion of Israel remains to be considered—the place that the thought of eternity held in it. It is generally asserted that existence after death, with all the ideas connected with it, was either unknown or denied in Mosaism. This assertion I venture emphatically to contradict. True, the rewards promised to good deeds, the punishments threatened against crimes, are all temporal, terrestrial. There is no mention of happiness or misery beyond the grave, but good reasons may be assigned for this reticence. Moses, in speaking to the people of the results of their conduct, speaks to them as a nation (Lev. xxvii.; Deut. xxviii.), and nations have no existence in a future world as individuals have; their whole lives are spent here; here on earth they "eat the fruit of their doings;" here and here only they enjoy the reward of their virtues and suffer the penalty of their vices.

Again, the condition of the nation of Israel was to be an illustration to all the world of the effects of righteousness and sin. Their worldly prosperity, their power and happiness, were to encourage other nations to godliness. Their disasters, their defeat, and their misery, were to deter other nations from falling into their backslidings. Hence all stress was laid on the *immediate* results of their actions.

Finally, the promise of future bliss, the threat of future wretchedness, is a terrible weapon when wielded by an unscrupulous priesthood. Researches into Egyptian history have shown how large a space the doctrine of immortality held in the cult of the ancient inhabitants of the Nile Valley, and what enormous power was usurped in consequence by the priestly caste. Roman Catholicism[1] in modern days furnishes another illustration of the same abuse. Dying men were terrified into bequeathing vast sums and large estates to the Church. Thus the clergy grew rich and powerful, while families were despoiled and the State impoverished. But the priests of Israel were to flourish with the prosperity of their people, not to fatten on their degradation and dependence. They were to hold no land, but to live on the offerings of those to whom they ministered.

For these reasons no distinct declaration is made concerning existence after death. But it is a mistake to imagine that no *allusion* is made to such an existence.

There is the injunction (Deut. xviii. 11) forbidding enquiring of the dead.

The term for death is "being gathered unto one's

---

[1] Compare Benisch's *Judaism Surveyed*, p. 38.

fathers," implying the thought of re-union of loved and loving ones after death.

God, forbidding to Noah and his sons murder and suicide, strengthens his prohibitions by the words: "Your blood of your *souls* will I require" (Gen. ix. 5); while in other books of the Bible the allusions to another state of existence are neither few nor obscure.

Thus briefly and imperfectly (for the subject demands a volume rather than a magazine article) have I sketched the ideas and practices which formed the religion of the nation rescued from Egypt and settled in Canaan, a religion that may rightly be named after him who took so large a share in the establishment of the nation—Mosaism.

Let us now proceed to enquire what modifications resulted from the terrible vicissitudes the people of Israel experienced—their repeated defeats and final overthrow as an independent nation, the destruction of their Temple, the loss of their country, their dispersion throughout the world, their persecution on every side, and lastly their re-admission into the ranks of humanity, a beneficent movement commenced not a century ago, and still very far from being universally accomplished.

1. From Babylon there returned to the land of Judah, with Ezra, a remnant poor in number and

in influence, but rich in religious zeal. The nation of Israel had passed through a fiery furnace; it came forth terribly reduced but greatly purified. We hear never again of idol worship in connection with Israel. Henceforth their belief in God's Unity, in God's Spirituality, reigns supreme.

Another characteristic of the restored nation, was an anxious desire to know and to perform all the institutions of the Law. There are passages scattered throughout the historical books which would lead us to suppose that, during the times of the Judges and the Kings, some of the most important laws were ignored or neglected. The great Festivals seem not to have been regularly observed. We know (2 Chron. xxxvi. 21) that the Sabbatical year was not kept as a period of rest for the land. During the Babylonian exile, of necessity the institution of sacrifices had fallen into desuetude.

Now began an earnest investigation, an almost feverish activity, to know the requirements of the Law in their entirety. All that remained of the ancient literature was sought out and put together, and gradually the Canon was formed. The Pentateuch was studied with an ardour not to be satiated. Believed to be inspired, it was thought that every word, letter, and point, had secret meanings, which would reveal themselves to the diligent student.

The memories of the aged were racked for details as to how institutions had been observed in olden times. The recollections of scholars were sought for as to the teachings of their departed instructors. And thus there grew up a mass of material, consisting of traditions and the results of original investigation, which afterwards became arranged as Mishna and Gemara, together forming the Talmud.

2. Thus centuries passed, during which the tendency became more and more pronounced to revive with increasing rigour and minuteness every institution of ancient Mosaism. A political crisis which seemed likely to arrest and subvert this tendency, did in the sequel only expedite and intensify it. The nation fell under the Grecian yoke, and a class —the governing class too—attracted by a learning, luxury, and refinement hitherto unknown to them, attracted too by the sensuous joys it held out to them—a class including even the High Priest—was ready to abandon the ancestral faith, and to adopt that of their conquerors. For imperial reasons in connection with his projected vengeance on Rome, Antiochus encouraged this disposition, and even attempted by savage enactments to drive the entire nation to follow their aristocratic leaders. But persecution generally produces results exactly opposite to those aimed at by it, and the Mac-

cabean uprising resulted not only in the throwing off of the Grecian yoke, but in the increase of attachment to the national religion and to those distinctive rites the Greeks had specially striven to efface.

Thus grew up Pharisaism, generally regarded as synonymous with all that was base, narrow-minded, and hypocritical, but which in truth was genuine religious ardour expressing itself in externals. Unfortunately externals alone are visible and imitable to the multitude, the spirit that animates and dignifies them is not so apparent nor so readily adopted.

At this epoch there arose the Great Teacher whose influence has so profoundly affected the world. He moved in Judea, filled with noble aspirations, denouncing mere formalities, impatient of all that fell short of His own high ideal. So far as I can perceive, His recorded words harmonise with what Isaiah, Jeremiah, or any Hebrew prophet taught concerning religion when they thundered against the follies or vices of their brethren. He lived and died an obedient son of Israel. Nor was His death the signal for the establishment of a new religion. His disciples, all born Jews, maintained Jewish institutions. It was not until forty years after, and then only under the influence of a vision (Acts x. 11-16), that Peter set aside the dietary laws. The Jewish Sabbath was long retained as the holy Day of Rest, and until the Gentiles in numbers gave ear to the preaching of the Apostles, the rite of circumcision was considered an essential qualification for Christianity, as it had been for Judaism. Indeed, it was Paul's preaching that authorised such departures from Jewish practice as constituted the establishment of a new faith, and from an historical point of view, I am inclined to name Paul rather than Jesus as the founder of the Christian religion.

During this period, and in the ages immediately succeeding, important changes took place in Judaism. The doctrine of life after death became prominent—now as belief in the resurrection of the body on the Day of Judgment, now in the more refined form of belief in the immortality of the soul. The Pharisees held both beliefs, the Sadducees (the Conservative party in Judaism) denied the former and were disposed to keep the latter in the background, hence they were popularly believed to reject altogether belief in a future state.

The development of the Messianic idea is another characteristic of this epoch. Every prophet had looked forward to a time when the fortunes of Israel should be triumphant, and the condition of man generally one of perfect peace and happiness, and most of the Hebrew seers had united with this glorious future the renewed splendour of the House of David. In times of material prosperity, as the need and so the desire for this future was less felt, the Messianic idea receded to the background. In times of gloom and disaster, and in proportion to the hopelessness of the present outlook, the Messianic idea became prominent, and its promises were passionately longed and prayed for. And to this day the Messianic idea is one of the most important and pregnant in Judaism, holding a chief place in its creed, and greatly influencing its ritual in every quarter of the globe—with this difference, that where the Jewish people are oppressed and trodden down, where their position is poor and degraded, there its special and personal features are most considered, there the Messiah is the earthly prince that will bring back Israel to Palestine, once more a great and powerful nation. Where the Jewish people possess religious liberty and civil rights, where they can enjoy without molestation the fruits of their labours, and find a fair field for the exercise of their talents, there the grander, the universal characteristics of the Messianic age are more regarded, and the coming of the Messiah means there the advent of the happy time when sin and want, war and misery, ignorance and superstition shall be no more.

One last and, perhaps, greatest change has to be considered, the change in the form of worship from sacrifice to prayer. While the second Temple still existed, certain prayers accompanied the sacrificial rites; but when the Temple was razed to the ground, and the Jewish people were cast forth to wander over the world, when it was no longer possible to present the prescribed offerings, then prayer became the only possible means whereby the Supreme could be publicly adored. Devotional compositions were prepared to be recited at the hours when the sacrifices had been offered. These compositions have increased as the ages have rolled on, but they are still grouped into services corresponding with the sacrifices offered daily and on special occasions.

Thus Judaism has maintained itself side by side with what, in connection with it, is often termed the daughter religion, but which, perhaps, should more correctly be termed its sister religion—Christianity; the one struggling for dear life against the suspicion and hate of the world, the other allied with greatness and power; once rivals, long foes, now and henceforth, it is to be hoped, friends and fellow-workers, differing in very important principles and practices, but holding in common other principles of priceless worth, proclaiming together God as the Father of all His children, striving together, though by different methods, to bring all men to the knowledge and worship of the Most High.

ISLAM AND CHRISTIANITY.

VII.

By Sir WILLIAM MUIR, Principal of Edinburgh University.

BEFORE proceeding to compare the teaching of Islam with that of the Gospel, one or two things may be mentioned on its relation to Judaism.

Built up as the religion was of materials borrowed mainly from the Jews, we should not be surprised at its assimilating more with the Mosaic Dispensation than with the Gospel, from which comparatively little was taken. Yet even from Judaism the divergence is very wide.

The Jews lived in constant anticipation of a future prophet and of a kingdom to come. Mahomet, on the other hand, announced himself the last of the prophets. As such, he is at once the Founder and the Finisher of the faith. The Jewish sentiment is expectation; the Moslem that of consummation. It was from Rabbinical sources, sacred and profane, that Mahomet took the greater part of his system, both doctrinal and ritualistic. Having taken what he wanted, he then brushed his authorities all aside. Nominally the prophets and their writings still remain objects of belief, but practically they are banished from sight, and nowhere to be found. The new revelation—the Coran and the Prophet's dicta—become thus the sole depository of Divine teaching. Professing to recognise "the previous Scriptures," Jewish and Christian, as inspired of God,—" a Light and Guide unto mankind"—Mahomet cast them all away, and they are to his followers practically as if they never had been. Thus the new Theology, though in theory a continuation of the Jewish and Christian Dispensations, took an altogether fresh point of departure. Unlike both the Jewish and Christian systems, it is founded exclusively on a single book, and on the authority and teaching of a single man.

In another matter,—that, namely, of religious warfare,—there might have been expected some consent of opinion between Judaism and Islam. In point of fact, there is none whatever. With the Israelites the command to fight had reference to the promised land from which alone the heathen were to be driven out; that accomplished, the command ceased and determined. The idea of fighting for the propagation of the law of Moses was unknown, either in the day of Joshua or at any subsequent era in Jewish history. With the Moslems, on the contrary, the propagation of Islam was the grand motive for drawing the sword. The command (though meant at first, it may be, only for Arabia) soon extended in ever-widening circles to the whole world. In one respect, indeed, the Moslem principle may seem more merciful than the Jewish; for the Arabian warriors were bidden first to call upon the nations to embrace Islam; and only on the failure of these to comply, were they to fight against them. Still, the effect on the national sentiment of the two peoples was as different as it possibly could be. If with the Jews there was the maxim, *Hate thine enemy*, it was in a sense common throughout the world, and never led to warfare for the aggrandisement of their religion. The command passed away with the occasion, and left none of its colouring behind.[1] With the Mahometans it ingrained itself as a leading element of their creed, and an abiding sentiment of national life.

---

[1] See Isaac Taylor in his *Spirit of the Hebrew Poetry*. "The Hebrew tribes did indeed enact the extermination of the Canaanitish races (so far as this was done), but the work of slaughter, done as it was, did not settle itself down in the national temper and habits, so as to show itself in the people as a permanent disposition." p. 132.

With them "warring in the ways of the Lord" was, and so remains, the highest kind of religious merit, bringing with it also the material reward of captive maids and riches upon earth, and for those falling on the battlefield, special blessedness with houris in the world to come. The soul of the Moslem is thus inflamed at once with the fire of fanaticism and the lust of plunder—sentiments with which the Jewish command failed to inspire the children of the conquerors of the Holy Land.

Points, moreover, of contrast with the Christian faith, both in doctrine, ritual and morals, meet us at every turn. And first as to Doctrine.

There is in Islam no mediator between God and man. The Deity, as conceived in the sense of severe unity, is approached immediately and directly. He is known as the just and sovereign Ruler of the Universe, whose special providence extends to the minutest concerns on earth, and who is the Hearer of prayer and the Judge of men and angels ;—but not as the Christian knows Him, "the Father in heaven ;"—fear thus with the Moslem worshipper rather than love predominating. Jesus is known historically as a Prophet; but He did not die; He was taken up into heaven. Sin may be forgiven; but it is so by the mere act of God— not for any merit's sake of a Redeemer. And the sanctifying work of the Holy Spirit is ignored altogether. Islam has not anything to put in place of these grand influences of grace and love by which the Christian's life is moulded and his heart constrained.

Next as to Ceremonial. Here everything is laid down by rule, and hence the tendency to mechanical performance. The round of ritual is prescribed and stereotyped. Prayer is divinely appointed to be said, with fixed rule of prostration and of genuflexion, at five stated periods of the day. One month for fasting every year is obligatory upon all, and is observed with singular rigour, day by day, from early dawn to sunset. The discipline is undoubtedly a severe exercise of self-denial, and of devotion to the faith; but its virtue is much neutralised by the indulgence allowed from sunset again till dawn of day, during which period restriction of every kind is withdrawn. Of similar tendency is the ordinance of Pilgrimage to Mecca and the neighbouring holy places—the tour terminated by the slaying of victims (the *Bairam* festival of the Turks),—a sacrificial custom like that of the Jews, but shorn of its Mosaic lesson. This pilgrimage is enjoined on all from every land who are possessed of the means to enter on it. All these solemnities are observed as works of merit in themselves, and also, no doubt, by many as means of religious elevation and improvement; but the tendency with the great mass of the Moslem world is towards the former end alone. Prayer, fasting, and pilgrimage, are services working out the salvation of the worshipper. No true believer can be lost, but if his bad deeds outweigh the good he must expiate the same in the life to come. On the other hand, heaven is drawn in the Coran in colouring of the most worldly and material hues. There are black-eyed virgins for wives, rich couches and carpets, fountains and cup-bearers of wine that exhilarates without inebriating—pictures these the sensuous tendencies of which must be to deaden the spiritual aspirations of the worshipper.

We turn now to the moral and social aspects of Islam. The relations established by the Coran between the sexes, will not compare with those of the Pentateuch, much less of the Gospel. Besides the privilege of having four free wives at a time, and of having as concubines any number of slaves he likes, the Moslem husband has by Divine law the power of divorcing the former at any moment and without any reason assigned. He is thus at liberty to "vary" even his married wives at his mere caprice and fancy. Social and domestic influences happily correct largely the abuse of this power. Nevertheless, that such is the license given by their Scripture cannot but have a deteriorating effect on the moral habitude of the people. Even in Mecca, for example, the citadel of the faith, there is enough to show the scandalous ebb to which in some quarters, without any transgression of the law, the sacred institution of marriage has fallen.

The jealous temperament of the Prophet provided restrictions on the liberty of women, not uncongenial to his followers, but materially affecting the position of the sex. They may be chastised, and they may be shut up in seclusion. They are forbidden to appear abroad without the veil, and stringent conditions are enjoined as to the admission into their rooms of any but the nearest relatives. All these depressing and unfriendly influences notwithstanding, woman, no doubt, retains by virtue of the remedial power of domestic life, a dominant, though it may be an uncertain, position within the harem or zenâna; but beyond its bounds her influence is well-nigh unknown. She is shut out from all the walks of outer life, and from all those sweet offices of mercy and philanthropy to which — but for the barrier of the Moslem revelation — she might, like her Jewish and Christian sisters, devote her life.

Nor is there hope of any effective amelioration. The law of the Coran is not, like the wide and adaptive inculcations of the Gospel, fitted for all time and for every onward movement of mankind. Its rule is hard and fast, a set of rigid ordinances incapable of change and relaxation. And thus, so long as the Coran prevails, woman remains secluded —her soft and purifying power lost upon the other sex outside the walls of the harem. It is the same with Slavery, the curse of Moslem lands. It cannot be eliminated from the law which the Mussulman holds to be Divine; it must continue to hold its place as an institution, casting a blight upon the proud slave-holder sadder even than on the poor victim of his pleasure.

It remains only now to notice the contrast to the teaching of the Gospel in the sphere of politics— namely, in the unity of the secular and spiritual elements forming the Moslem theory of government. Church and state are integrally one. The head of the state is head also of the faith; and the fusion runs throughout. The functions are synonymous. With the armies of Islam, for instance, which overran the world, the *Ameer*, or chief commander, as such, led also the prayers of his force. The spiritual function was badge also of secular and military supremacy. In theory Islam is a theocracy, originating in the Caliphate, or succession from the Prophet; and when the Caliphate passed away, breaking up into separate polities, the head of each of which is at once its secular and its ecclesiastical ruler. The result of such a system is that the chief must by necessity be absolute sovereign—a despot in the proper sense of the term. His power is only limited by the patience of the people, though also in a manner by the *Futwas* (theological and legal deliverances) of the Ulema and Doctors, which as Vicegerent of the Prophet the sovereign is bound to follow. The outcome of all this is that freedom, in the political sense of the word, is unknown. Liberal institutions, in which the people can take their share, and through which they may give effect to their collective wish, are altogether foreign to the genius of Islam, and under the *régime* of the Coran beyond the scope of expectation.

In fine, the fatal demerit of Islam, viewed in its social and political aspect, is that, tied and encrusted round as it is by the text of the Coran, progress and adaptation to varying circumstance are unattainable. Institutions based on the sanction of a revelation held to be divinely given are unalterable; they present a bar impassable to social and political amelioration. Elsewhere the world may advance; Islam, with its polity and law, as

Mahomet left them twelve centuries ago, remains the same.

It is hardly necessary to point out the difference of Christian teaching in respect of the various points enumerated above. They will, no doubt, have suggested themselves to the reader who may have been kindly giving his attention as he went along. For example, the Gospel, though holding the wife subject to the husband, has not the less implanted principles which now culminate in the elevation of the sex to a position of virtual equality. The social rules of the Bible possess a plastic virtue suitable for every race and clime and time. In place of the veil and restrictions on social intercourse, it simply enjoins modest apparel and "chaste conversation." And so, while altogether shut out from her legitimate influence on Moslem society, woman takes her place with us in all the walks of mercy and benevolence. She sheds the light and grace upon the world which the female sex alone can give, and the absence of which keeps Moslem life outside the harem austere and dark.

Not less marked is the contrast to the political environments of Islam. The doctrine of a common Father in heaven has opened the way to universal freedom. The captive, as "a brother beloved," at last is set at liberty; while the ordinance of slavery must prevail so long as the scripture of Mahomet is law. So also with political progress. Cæsar and the Church are free to go each its own way, and thus advance is possible on either side. The Gospel sheds its approval on every step of moral and social progress, if it do not indeed actually point out the way thereto.

And finally, instead of the cold lesson of morality which is all that Islam offers, with its fixed round of prayer, fasting, and pilgrimage, we have the warm and constraining influences of a faith and love which the personal sacrifice of a Redeemer alone can give;—

"In this was manifested the love of God toward us, because that God sent His only begotten Son into the world, that we might live through Him.

"Herein is love, not that we loved God, but that He loved us, and sent His Son to be the propitiation for our sins.

"Beloved, if God so loved us, we ought also to love one another."[1]

In this consists the sovereign virtue of the Gospel. We should search in vain for like virtue anywhere in the Coran or in the teaching of Mahomet.

[1] 1 John iv. 9-11.

BUDDHISM AND CHRISTIANITY.

VIII.

T. W. RHYS DAVIDS, LL.D., Ph.D., Barrister-at-Law, and Author of "Buddhism," "The Hibbert Lectures," 1881, etc.

ONE of the principal advantages of the great progress made in recent years in our knowledge of Buddhism is the opportunity which it affords for the comparison of our own civilisation with one which is altogether independent of it. To compare Biblical Theology with Mohammedanism is to compare it with a weak and modern system, the best parts of which are an inadequate and inaccurate reproduction, and that not immediately, but at second hand, from Biblical Theology itself. And to compare it with the popular religions, or philosophical systems of Greece and Rome, is to compare it with modes of thought which are very intimately connected, both by action and reaction, with itself. There has been, it is true, no little wild talk about the borrowings of Christianity from Buddhism.

But there has not as yet been discovered the slightest scintilla of evidence for any historical connection between the two. And the more we know about Buddhism the more clearly does it appear that the supposed resemblances are either due to passages in Buddhist books, which are post-Christian in date, or are only of the most superficial character. The fact is, that Buddhism is the most different from Christianity of all the great religions. Its fundamental conceptions are not only distinct from, but are in absolute contradiction to those of the Bible. And it is precisely on that account that the study of Buddhism is by far more instructive and interesting, from the comparative point of view, than any other of the systems that have been dealt with in this Symposium.

Many streams unite to form the religious conceptions of India. The main stream is that of Aryan thought, into which, from a very early date, there continually flowed not a few tributaries from the ideas of the non-Aryan peoples whom the Aryans gradually overcame in their progress down the valley of the Ganges. It would be impossible, within the limits of this short paper, to attempt to differentiate, in any detail, between these various constituents of Hinduism as it existed at the time of the rise of Buddhism, five hundred years before the birth of Christ. But the evolution of theology had followed among the Indian Aryans very much the same lines as it had followed among the Greeks, and had reached, at the time of which we speak, much the same result as had been reached at the same time by the Aryans in Europe.

Ethics and theology were as yet distinct. All mysteries in Nature were explained by the action of spirits. Among the innumerable spirits on the earth and in the sky, a few, the personifications of the more striking natural events, had been raised to the rank of great gods. And the pantheistic philosophers had already dimly supposed a unity behind the multiplicity of these spiritual hypotheses, and had postulated a first cause, a god whom they called Brahmá, as the one being of whom all other spirits, and all men, and animals, and things, were but the temporary and changing forms. With these speculations, and even with the great gods, the mass of the people did not much concern themselves. They were great believers in all kinds of lucky signs and dreams and omens. They worshipped all kinds of local or tribal gods with the object of averting misfortune or gaining wealth. They believed in the existence of spirits or souls inside their own bodies, and in a kind of shadowy future life for those souls after their bodies had died. And such existence would be happy or the reverse, not so much in consequence of their conduct in life, as in consequence of certain ceremonies being performed or not at the time of their death.

Meanwhile, side by side with these theological or spiritual ideas, but quite independent of them, there had been gradually forming a set of elementary ethical ideas—life, except that of enemies, or of animals required for food, was not to be taken. There were limitations as regards marriage, and the chastity of any woman under the protection of other men was carefully respected. The rights of individual property had been already acknowledged, and there was an elaborate code of customary rules with regard to communal property. Great stress was laid on reverence to elders, on etiquette, and on ceremonial behaviour. Gratitude, kindness, generosity, and of course bravery, were held in high esteem. And the caste system, already in full vogue, involved a number of carefully balanced rights and duties.

The next stage in the ordinary course of things would have been for some reformer to amalgamate the results of ethical and of theological thought into a new pantheistic or theistic religion—religion, that is, in the modern sense, a guide not only to belief about spirits, but also to right conduct. The peculiarity of Gotama's reform lay in this: that he ignored and despised the whole of the theology, and after elaborating, refining, and enlarging the ethics, made them alone the basis of a new system entirely independent of all the previous spirit hypotheses.

He considered, and deliberately condemned as vague speculation—not only useless but inimical to righteousness of life—the idea of a personal God as the first cause and immanent reality of all things. He considered, and deliberately condemned as vain speculation — injurious to character or to any growth in goodness — the idea of a soul as the eternal substratum of the individual life of men. He considered, and deliberately condemned as vain, immoral, and weak, the prevalent idea that the salvation of the soul could be ultimately attained by a happy life in heaven. It would be superfluous to compare such conclusions with Biblical Theology. May we not rather ask whether it would be possible to formulate any system which should be in more absolute and categorical contradiction to all the bases of Christian belief?

The further question now arises whether the ethics of the Buddhist scriptures, the positive aspects of Gotama's teaching, stand in the same violent contrast to Christian ethics as the Buddhist views of God and the soul do to Biblical Theology? Partly yes and partly no. The Buddhist theory distinguishes the morality of the ordinary unconverted man from that of the converted man, the sotápanno, who has entered on the excellent way. With regard to the former the resemblances are sometimes, no doubt, very close. But they are also, for the purposes of our present enquiry, very unimportant. It is inaccurate to quote such resemblances as evidence of any anticipation of Christian by Buddhist ethics. They have in reality very little to do either with the one or with the other. And Buddhist ethics, to be rightly understood or judged, must be considered from the point of view of the higher morality of the converted man.

The Buddhist salvation was held to consist in a certain state of mind to be gained and enjoyed in this present life, and not extending beyond the grave. This state of mind is occasionally in the Buddhist books called Nirvána, or "the going out," and meaning the going out in the heart of the three fires of lust, ill-will, and foolishness. This name of the blissful state I refer to first as it is the one exclusively used in English works on the subject of Buddhism. But in the Buddhist books it is only one out of many epithets of the perfect rest of Arahatship. Others are Freedom, Purity, Holiness, Bliss, Happiness, the End of Suffering, the Cessation of Craving, Peace, Calm, Tranquillity, the Other Shore, the Island of Refuge, Emancipation, the Cessation (of human passion), the Secure, the Cave, the Supreme, the Transcendent, the Formless, the Truth, the Imperishable, the Infinite, Ambrosia, the Immaterial, the Abstract, the Uncreated, the Unseen, the Ineffable, the Sorrowless, Detachment, the Fruit (of the path of Arahatship), and many others. Each of these terms is used quite absolutely, without any qualifying expression, and many of them would require a commentary to make their full connotation plain. Some of them are used quite as frequently as that epithet of "the going out," which has been selected by European writers, and the Pali words for them would be quite as accurate a name for the Buddhist ideal state. More frequent than any is, however, the expression Arahatship, "the state of him who is worthy," and that word, therefore, is the one that will be used in the remainder of this paper.

Now Arahatship is best defined, both from the positive side and the negative, by an enumeration of the various things which are to be included or excluded by the state of mind of the Arahat. In the first place, he is one who has traversed the so-called Excellent Way, which consists of eight divisions or categories :—

1. Right Views — free from superstition or delusion.

2. Right Desires—such inclinations, aspirations, as lead a man to choose the right.

3. Right Speech—kindly, open, truthful.

4. Right Conduct—peaceful, honest, pure.

5. Right Livelihood—bringing hurt or danger to no living thing.

6. Right Effort—in self-training and in self-control.

7. Right Mindfulness—the ever active mind, watchful and alert.

8. Right Rapture—the ecstasy which follows an earnest contemplation of the deep mysteries of life.

This division, due to Gotama himself, is supplemented by another, also due to the founder of Buddhism, in which the Excellent Way is divided into four stages; each of these stages consisting in the breaking of certain bonds or chains by which the unconverted are bound.

In the first, the stage of Conversion, the disciple gets rid of delusions regarding the permanency and importance of his own individuality. The breaking of this bond is the entrance upon the excellent way. It is the breaking away from self, the self-renunciation, which is held to be the foundation of all righteousness.

The next step (in the same stage) is the destruction of Doubt. When the eyes of the disciple are open to the insignificance and the impermanency of his own being, he must not, therefore, give up hope, and think that all is lost. By faith in the victory already achieved by the great Arahat, the Buddha himself, over the powers of evil; by faith in the efficacy of the excellent way pointed out by him for the destruction of sorrow, he must overcome all doubt, and proceed, full of assurance of his ultimate success (for those who have once entered the path can never lose it, can never fail), to the next step.

This is the getting rid of the bond called "Belief in the efficacy of rites and ceremonies, ascetic practices, and mere outward works of worldly morality." It is the perception of the only *method* by which the disciples can hope for salvation. The first part of it is a protest against the benefits supposed to result from the ritual prescribed by the Brahmins, and from all those ascetic practices which have been so popular in India. But it probably includes also in its condemnation, any worship in any manner of any spiritual power or being.[1] The second part, based on the destruction above pointed out, is an inculcation of the necessity of "inwardness," of a real change of heart, and is the Buddhist analogue to the long vexed battle between faith and works so hotly waged between Christian writers.

When the disciple whose eyes have been opened has thus renounced self, is full of faith, and has grasped the right method to be followed in the struggle, his conversion is complete, and he is sure of attaining to Arahatship, either in his present, or in some future birth.

The next two stages are entirely occupied with the struggle against the three deadly enemies of the religious life—Lust, Ill-will, and Dulness. I must call attention to the fact—it is the only bit of controversy that has been allowed to intrude upon our narrow space—that it is lust, and not desire, which is the chain or bond to be broken. It is a common blunder in English treatises on Buddhism that the Buddhist scriptures, or Gotama himself, inculcated the extinction of desire. There

---

[1] The worship of the "Great Being," the one god of Brahmin speculation, is expressly forbidden in the Brahma Jála Sulla, I., 26, among a list of vain ceremonies, including astrology and witchcraft! And the reference there is not to the righteousness of the Arahat, but only to the lower morality of the Sílas.

is not one passage in the Buddhist books to support so absurd a contention. Lusts, craving, longing, excitement, greed, all that lies at the root of that unworthy scramble for wealth or power or social position so characteristic of the un-Christian life of modern Christian cities, is undoubtedly condemned in many passages; and is even stated, under the frequent simile of burning thirst, to be the ultimate cause of all sorrow. But the cultivation of right desires is an essential part of Buddhist ethics.

The destruction of the second of these three bonds, Ill-will, is to be brought about by the cultivation of the opposite quality of Love, and that not to men only, but to animals and gods. "As a mother, even at the risk of her own life, protects her son, her only son, so let him (the Arahat) cultivate good-will without measure towards all beings: let him cultivate a heart of love that knows no measure, and that knows no stint, unobstructed by any sense of differing or opposing interests, towards the whole world above, below, around!"[1] When the disciple has reached the end of this stage of the excellent way he will attain to Arahatship in his next birth. This is the only place found in the higher Buddhist ethics

[1] Sutta Nipáta, I., 8, 7.

for love to God; and even then the words are not used in any Christian sense. "The Great Being" is only Brahmá, and the love is not the filial love of a father.

By the third of this evil trio, Dulness, is not of course meant dulness in the modern sense, want of excitement, but dulness in a peculiar Buddhist sense, want of impressibility to higher things, that spiritual deadness to the higher life which would prevent the disciple from progressing in his struggle, in his journey along the excellent way. And with the complete victory over this "dulness" the disciple has reached the end of the first half of the path.

The latter half is occupied with the breaking of bonds, considered, in Buddhist ethics, to be even more difficult to get free from than the evil trio just explained. These new foes are, firstly, the desire for future life, either on earth or in heaven; and, secondly, the desire for future life in the immaterial worlds beyond. It is strange that with this injunction on the very threshold of Buddhist ethics there should still be popular writers who describe the Buddhist ideal as an absorption into nothing. I very much doubt whether any man at any time or place can ever have held any such ideal. There were, no doubt, isolated Brahmin thinkers in the time of Gotama who desired a future life in an immaterial world. And this might possibly be described, but inaccurately, loosely, and inadequately, as an absorption into nothing. Now even any such desire is here expressly declared to be, not only not a part of, but incompatible with the Buddhist ideal life of Arahatship.

The third and fourth of these tighter bonds are, like the first and second, closely allied. They are Pride and Self-righteousness, which are to be overcome by the cultivation of the opposite virtues of humility and reverence for others. And the last enemy to be conquered, the last bond to be broken, is Ignorance, considered, in Buddhist ethics, to be the most deadly obstacle to the attainment of religious perfection. This word, also, is here used in a technical sense. It was not simply ignorance of history, or science, or any worldly wisdom, but rather, ignorance of the Four Noble Truths, and other similar fundamental points in religious knowledge and insight.

I have gone thus far into detail regarding Arahatship, not only because it is the central and most fundamental part of Buddhist ethics, but because a knowledge of those details will enable any reader of this paper to understand at once and without any further discussion, precisely the degree in which Buddhist ethics do, and still more do not agree with Christian ethics. The conclusion may, I think, be summed up somewhat in this way.

We find scattered throughout the Bible a number of passages describing the ideal character, or pointing out mental or spiritual dispositions, qualities, which it should, on the one hand, include, and on the other hand, exclude. It is true that these statements are not systematised, and that different writers, or occasionally the same writers in different passages, seem to lay different stress on some one side rather than on some other side of the ideal Christian character. This is partly because of the importance attached rather to the spirit than the letter, partly because the necessary space is occupied with other matters, partly because of the way in which the Bible was formed. We find, in consequence, that the great fathers and leaders of the Christian Church do not always take precisely the same view of the Christian character. But the picture drawn in the sacred writings is very sufficiently clear as a whole, and the differences of interpretation either deal with minor points, or consist in the greater prominence given to some portion of the doctrine held after all, though in less degree, by opposing theologians.

On comparing this ideal with the Buddhist Arahatship (or Nirvána), we find a not inconsiderable number of what may fairly be called resemblances, but of what I think it would be more accurate to call points of contact. Some of these are in such elementary matters as truthfulness, honesty, chastity, kindliness. Others have relation to the deeper side of the religious life, and one or two of these are strange coincidences. The importance attached to conversion, to a change of heart, to self-renunciation, to inwardness, to faith, to humility, and to love, are of the essence of ethics. Such coincidences as that of the final perseverance of the saints, of the peace which passeth understanding, of the absolute consciousness of the victory won, of the position taken in the controversy as to faith and works, are striking. And the feeling of the New Testament as to wealth, and the feeling of many Christians as to preference, in the highest religious life of all, for the unmarried over the married life, might be matched with passages from the Buddhist scriptures. But a critical examination of any one of these resemblances would show that in no single instance are the ideas identical. They are at most analogous. The words are never used in precisely the same sense. They are wrapped up with implications, connotations, which are always more or less present to the minds of the Buddhists who use them. The ideas themselves, therefore, expressed in the words are not the same, and we have to deal, not with any real agreement, but only with points of contact.

Another matter to which considerable importance is often attached (but which is really a question, neither of theology nor of ethics, but of literature), is that the terms of expression, or the similes employed in the Buddhist texts, are sometimes strangely suggestive of other texts more familiar to us. Thus we find parables of the sower, of the mustard seed, and of the two mites, a set of very beautiful beatitudes,[1] a section (or chapter) on the treasure laid up in the inward man which no thief can steal. We are told how it is bad actions and not the eating of so-called unclean foods, which defile a man, and how the wages of sin is death. There is a frequently recurring phrase, "in the spirit and not in the letter." Arahatship is obtained without money and without price. The Arahat is described as dead to the world, while at the same time he is not to hide his light, but so to let it shine forth that others may profit. Of the

---

[1] One of the blessed states, by the way, being "having right desires in the heart."

ascetics it is said in condemnation that "within thee there is ravening, while the outside thou makest clean." And we have the whole armour of the Buddhist, with uprightness as the cloak, and meditation as the breastplate, watchfulness as the shield, insight as the spear, the Word as the sword, the threefold wisdom as the crest of the helmet, and the fruit of the excellent way (that is, Arahatship or Nirvána) as the jewel at its summit. One might go on quoting such passages indefinitely or point out phrases in the Buddhist writings which could be transferred to Christian sermons. But in no case does the analogy really run on all fours, nor could any serious argument be founded on the apparent identity of expression, or the suggested similarity of thought.

For—and here we come to the gist of the matter—it is precisely those ideas in the Bible which are most instinctively and specially Christian, which are not only wanting in, but are *absolutely contradicted in, Buddhism.* In it we have an ethical system but no lawgiver, a world without a Creator, *a salvation without eternal life,* and a sense of evil, but *no conception of pardon, atonement, reconciliation, or redemption.* To a Christian the world, though a vale of tears, is after all the Father's world; and the powers of sin and evil, though mighty, are as nothing when compared with the omnipotence of a reconciled Father. The Buddhist reverences the Buddha as the best and the wisest of men, the king of righteousness who has led the way to victory. But the Christian worships the Son of God, who is at the same time the Son of Man, the Divine Man, with that unspeakable love and adoration which are due to Him for His incarnation and atoning death upon the cross. To the Christian life and immortality are brought to light by the Gospel; by the Buddhist an immortal life is not only conceived as impossible, but *would be looked upon as a disaster*. These are essential matters. It is in such that not merely divergence but contradiction is visible at every step. And they really colour all those points of contact which seem to show, at first sight, a *superficial* resemblance. Thus the Buddhist humility is not humility before God, the Buddhist peace is *not* the peace of God, and the *Buddhist wisdom is ignorance of God*.

In the foregoing analysis I have only endeavoured, as clearly and accurately as possible, to compare the Buddhism of the Buddhist scriptures with Biblical theology. The history of Buddhism is the history of the greater half of the civilised world for nearly two and a half millenniums; the history of Christianity is the history of the other half for nearly two millenniums. To compare all Buddhism with all Christianity would be a colossal, perhaps an impossible task. And no attempt has been made to touch upon the points of contact between the Gospels and the Buddhist lives of the Buddha. Those who wish to see a full discussion of this latter subject, will find it in the elaborate work of Professor Seydel, of Leipsic.

But perhaps the most instructive part of a comparative study of Buddhism, is to be found in the astounding fact that the ethical revolution of Gotama, the stately bridge which he has attempted to build over the sorrow of the world, has led to the establishment of a papal hierarchy holding views as far apart from the subtle and deep-reaching doctrine of the Excellent Way, as Roman Ultramontanism is from the simplicity of the Gospel. It is true that the resemblances here also are more apparent than real. But it is none the less instructive that a system in many respects so true and so beautiful that Dr. Reynolds says of its founder,[1] "Verily our Lord would have said of Gotama, 'Thou art not far from the kingdom of God,'" should have ended in Lámáism, its shaven

---

[1] In "Buddhism: a comparison and a contrast between Buddhism and Christianity;" published by the Religious Tract Society, p. 64.

priests, its bells and rosaries and images and holy water, its services in surpliced robes with double choirs and processions and mystic rites and incense, its abbots and monks and nuns of many grades, its worship of the double Virgin and of saints and angels, its huge monasteries, its gorgeous cathedrals, its powerful hierarchy, its cardinals, and above all, its pope with a tiara on his head, and thought to be the incarnation and vicegerent of a spiritual power in the skies.

Are we to suppose that this marvellous coincicidence is due to a miracle (or rather to ten thousand miracles)? or are we to conclude that in such matters similar causes acting, quite independently, under similar conditions will produce similar results?

ANCIENT SCANDINAVIAN RELIGION.

IX.

By the Hon. RASMUS B. ANDERSON, Minister of the United States, Denmark, and Author of "Norse Mythology," "America not discovered by Columbus," &c.

IN the forces and phenomena of Nature we must look for the origin of the heathen mythologies. Thus the shepherds found their gods in the bright stars that twinkled every night, and seemed to whisper to them of secrets which they could not themselves divine and of powers they did not know. Thus when the Norsemen heard the thunder roll and saw the lightning-flash crushing everything in its way, there came to them an image of a mighty god who rode in his chariot athwart the heavens with such din and crash, and so fast that his path was wrapped in flames.

The two European mythologies best known to us are the Greek and the Scandinavian. As widely as Greeks differ from the Scandinavians, so widely is Scandinavian mythology different from the Greek. The chief end sought by the Greeks was beauty and harmony. Fostered beneath a clear sky and a sun that never scorches, in a climate where north winds never pierce, the Greek cherished beauty in his soul and fashioned gods and goddesses remarkable for their sweetness and grace. But in the ice-bound regions of the North, where the long arms of the glaciers clutch the valleys in their cold embrace, and the death-portending avalanches cut their way down the mountain sides, the people dwelt with a peculiar intensity of feeling upon the tragedy of Nature. From childhood the Norsemen were trained to strife, and thus a race was developed fond of rocking on the stormy seas and of reddening the keen sword-edge in the blood of the foe—and hence their gods became strong and warlike. The old Norsemen cared but little for quiet harmony and beauty. Theirs were the valkyries who rode through the air and hovered over the battlefield to select the heroes who were to fall and be carried to Odin, there to fight again until the world should perish in Ragnarok.

The ancient Scandinavians cannot be said to have possessed any clearly-defined knowledge of a god outside of Nature—that is, of any Supreme God. Their highest divinity was Odin, the father of gods and men, as he is styled. He occupies a position like that of Zeus in Greek mythology. Still there are passages both in the Eddas and in the Sagas which more or less vaguely point to a god outside of Nature and higher than Odin. In the lay of Hyndla, in the Elder Edda, we find this striking passage :—

> Then one is born
> Greater than all;
> He becomes strong
> With the strengths of earth;
> The mightiest king
> Men call him,
> Fast knit in peace
> With all powers.
>
> Then comes another
> Yet more mighty;
> *But him dare I not*
> *Venture to name:*
> Few further may look
> Than to where Odin
> To meet the wolf goes.

Odin we know "goes to meet the wolf" (that is, the Fenriswolf), in Ragnarok, in the final conflict between all good and evil powers, and thus the poet has here referred to an unknown or nameless god, just as the Greeks, according to Paul, had an altar with the inscription: TO THE UNKNOWN GOD. It was of this same unknown god that one of the ancient Greek poets had said that in him we live, and move, and have our being. Thus just as the Greeks found in the labyrinth of their heathen deities a god greater than Zeus, so the Supreme God, superior to Odin, stands out, though less distinctly, in the Scandinavian heathen belief.

And in accordance with this statement we find that this "yet more mighty one" whom the rhapsodist "dare not venture to name" is worshipped by various old and thoughtful men in the pre-Christian age. I will mention a few examples.

It is recorded that Ingemund the Old, a heathen Norseman in Iceland, bleeding and dying, prayed the nameless god to forgive his murderer, Rolleif.

Thorkel Maane, a supreme judge of Iceland in the heathen time, a man of unblemished life, and distinguished as a most wise magistrate, declared that he would worship no other God than Him who had created the sun, and in his dying hour he prayed the Father of Light to illuminate his soul in the darkness of death. It is related that when Thorkel Maane had arrived at the age of maturity and reflection he refused a blind obedience to traditionary custom, and employed much of his time in weighing the established tenets of his countrymen by the standard of reason. He divested his mind of all prejudice; he pondered on the sublimity of Nature, and guided himself by maxims founded on truth and good sense. By these means he discovered not only the fallacy of the asafaith, but also became a convert to the belief in the existence of a power more mighty than Odin or Thor. In his Creator he recognised his God and to Him alone directed his worship, from a conviction that none other was worthy to be honoured and adored. On perceiving the approach of death this pious man asked to be conveyed into the open air in order that, as he said, he might in his last moments contemplate the glories of the great God who had made the earth and the heavens and all that in them is.

One more example will suffice. Harold Fairhair, the first sovereign of Norway, the king who united Norway under his sceptre in the year 872, was accustomed to assist at the public offerings made by the people in honour of their gods. As none other than the Odinic religion was known in that country in their days, he acted with prudence in not betraying either contempt or disregard for the prevailing worship of the land, lest his subjects, stimulated by such example, might become indifferent, not only to their sacred, but also to their political duties. Yet in his heart of hearts he rejected those superstitious ceremonies, and believed in the existence of a more powerful divinity whom he secretly worshipped. "I swear," he once said, "never to make my offerings to an idol, but to that God alone whose omnipotence has formed the world and stamped man with His own image. It would be an act of folly in me to expect help from him whose power and empire arises from the accidental hollow of a tree or the peculiar form of a stone."

All will agree that every mythology embodies some religious faith. Just as we at the present time seek to find God by philosophical speculation (natural theology), by our emotional nature, by our good deeds, or by all these at one time, and just as we, when we have found Him, rest upon His breast, although we do not fully agree as to our conception of Him, each one of us having his own god as each has his own rainbow, so the heathens of old sought God everywhere—in the rocks, in the babbling stream, in the heavy ear of grain, in the star-strewn sky of night, and in the splendour of the sun. To interpret a myth therefore is not only to give its source but also its aim, together with the thoughts and feelings it awakened in the human breast.

Many writers have claimed that the Scandinavian mythology is a degradation of and aberration from the Biblical religion. They take the position that there was originally one tongue and one religion. Viewed from this standpoint the two Eddas of Iceland are a sort of Old and New Testament, which have come down to us through vast ages, growing, as traditions do, continually more obscure, and accumulating lower matter and more divergent and more pagan doctrines, as the walls of old castles become covered with mosses and lichens, till they finally assume the form in which they were collected from the lips of the Norsemen and put in a permanent written form. Interpreters of this school claim that through all mythologies there run certain great lines which converge toward one common centre, and point to an original source of a religious faith which has grown dimmer and more disfigured the further it has gone. They say Central Asia is the geographical centre from which all the systems of heathen belief have proceeded. Upon this theory Loke of the Scandinavians, Pluto of the Greeks, Ahriman of the Persians, Siva of the Hindoos, &c., are all originally the devil of the Bible, who has changed his name and, more or less, his personal form and characteristics. The Scandinavian Odin, Vile, and Ve; Odin, Hœner, and Loder; and Odin, Thor, and Bilder, are degenerated representatives of the Biblical Trinity. There are scholars even at the present day who find in the Scandinavian cosmogony, in a somewhat mutilated and interpolated condition, the Biblical story of the creation, preservation, destruction, and regeneration of this world. Ygdrasil, the wonderful ash-tree of existence, is the Tree of Life in the Garden of Eden. Ask and Embla, the first human pair, are Adam and Eve; the blood of the slain giant Ymer, in which the whole race of frost giants was drowned, excepting one pair who were saved in a skiff and from whom a new giant race descended, is made to represent the deluge. The citadel called Midgard is the Tower of Babel. In the death of Balder, slain by Hoder, who was instigated by Loke, is found the crucifixion of Christ slain by Judas, who was instigated by the devil. The heaven and hell so vividly described in the Eddas furnish a large field for comparison with Biblical passages on the same subjects. The trouble with these interpreters is that they attempt to prove too much. It is in our judgment sufficient to say that races which can trace their languages to a common origin have also got their religious systems from a common source. We know that the Aryan or Indo-European languages converge into one in the dim past, and consequently we assume that the Aryan religions flow from a common original spring. But so long as no scholar has demonstrated that Greek or Norse are originally the same language as Hebrew, there is no good reason for assuming that Ask and Embla are merely Norse names for Adam and Eve.

On the other hand, just as we have many Semitic words incorporated in the English tongue, and just as Aryan words have found their way into Hebrew, so Scandinavian Mythology has been more or less influenced by Christian ideas after the two systems of religion met and came in contact with each other. And who denies that the Christian Church has borrowed much from the various mythologies of Europe? In the present customs of the European peoples much of the old heathenism is preserved. Nay, we might almost say that the whole Odinic mythology still exists, not as a faith and doctrine, but as a form of worship adapted to Christianity. The old great Scandinavian festivals with their various ceremonies have simply been converted into Christian festivals. This is true of Christmas, which the old Norseman called Yule; and is not the Christmas tree a survival of the ash-tree Ygdrasil? The festivals of Easter, of St. John, and of St. Michael are old Scandinavian festivals Christianised. In many instances, even the places of worship were retained. Where a heathen divinity had long been worshipped, the Christians built a church and dedicated it to some saint or other, to whom, henceforth, both the worship and the myth were referred and became blended.

St. Michael took the place of Odin or Thor, and the Odin or Thor myths were henceforth told of St. Michael. Where there was a tree sacred to Odin, an image of St. Mary was hung up, but in other respects the old form of worship was continued under the protection of the Church. Of course the customs have taken a stronger hold on the Catholic Church, while Protestants have allowed many of them to pass into disuse. What we mean to emphasise is simply the fact that while Scandinavian mythology doubtless borrowed much from the Christian religion, and in turn lent much to it, the two systems are essentially different, and there is no evidence of a common original source.

As already indicated, Scandinavian mythology must look for its fundamental interpretation in physical Nature. The divinities are the forces and phenomena of Nature personified. The works of the gods correspond faithfully to the events and scenes of the outward world. But we must not neglect to apply an ethical or spiritual explanation as well. The spiritual and physical interpretation must be combined. In other words, we must regard the gods as as human as possible. The phenomena and forces of nature were personified by the ancient Scandinavians into deities and the myths were elaborated to suit the moral, intellectual, and emotional nature—the inner life of man. The deities were conceived in human form, with human attributes and affections. The ancient Scandinavians depicted themselves in their gods, and so clothed them with their own faculties of mind and body in respect to good and evil, virtue and vice, right and wrong. Read what the great Norse scholar Rudolf Keyser has said on this point:—

"The gods are the ordaining powers of Nature clothed in personality. They direct the world which they created; but beside them stand the mighty goddesses of fate and time, the great norns, who sustain the world-structure, the all-embracing tree of the world, that is Ygdrasil. The life of the world is a struggle between the good and the light gods on the one side, and the offspring of chaotic matter, the giants, Nature's disturbing forces, on the other. This struggle extends also into man's being: the spirit proceeds from the gods, the body belongs to the world of the giants. They struggle with each other for the supremacy. If the spirit conquers by virtue and bravery, man goes to heaven after death to fight in concert with the gods against the evil powers; but if the body conquers and

K

links the spirit to itself by weakness and low desires, then man sinks after death to the world of the giants in the lower regions, and joins himself with the evil powers in the warfare against the gods."

Nature is the mother at whose breast we are all nourished. In ancient times she was the object of child-like contemplation and adoration. The contemplation of the heavens produced the myth about Odin, and the thunder-storm suggested Thor, as in the Greek mythology Argos with his hundred eyes represents the star-lit heavens, and the wandering Io whom Hera had set him to watch is the wandering moon. But stopping here would be too prosaic. It would be giving the empty shell and throwing away the kernel. The old Frisians regarded the world as a huge ship called Maningfual, a counterpart to the Scandinavian ash Ygdrasil. The mountains were its masts. The captain must go from one place to another of the ship to give his orders on horseback. The sailors go aloft as young men to make sail, and when they arrive down again their hair and beard are white. Ay, are we not all sailors on board this great ship, and have we not all enough to do, each in his own way, to climb its ropes and ladders, and make and reef its sails, and do not our hairs turn grey ere we are aware of it? But take the human element out of these myths, and what is there left of them?

The sources to be examined in regard to Scandinavian mythology are many and varied. Throughout the Scandinavian countries are found monumental stones on which Runic inscriptions have been written in heathen times. Of these "Runic Monuments," no less than three folio volumes have been published by the great and indefatigable scholar and runologist, Professor George Stephens of Copenhagen.

From heathen Germany we have a few ancient laws and a few glossaries containing mythological words. The *Lex Salica*, of which we have a Latin translation, was doubtless originally produced in the German tongue. In the time of Chlodevig it was translated into Latin, and here and there words from the original text were inserted parenthetically, to guarantee, as it were, the correctness of the version. But in course of time these words were either wholly omitted or greatly corrupted by transcribers. Then there are formulæ by which the new converts to Christianity renounced the old gods, and in which names of heathen divinities therefore occur. But precious though it be, the amount of mythological information to be gathered from these and similar sources is very small. A richer vein of information is the tolerably well represented collection of German heroic poems, among which the most important are the Niblung story and Gudrun. The Heliand preserves a number of heathen phrases and figures of speech. The Anglo-Saxon Beowulf poem would be more valuable had not the Christian transcriber conceived it to be his duty to omit the names of the heathen gods occurring in the lay.

Iceland, that wonderful island of the cold and boisterous North Sea, is the Mecca to which all they must turn who would understand the Odinic religion. Iceland is the Patmos where the Apocalypse of the Teutonic race was recorded. Here we find the well of Mimer and the fountain of Urd. In Icelandic we find a whole library of mythological literature, put in writing after the introduction of Christianity (A.D. 1000), and after the people had adopted the Roman alphabet, but still written in the spirit of the asafaith, "naught extenuating and putting down naught in malice." The most important of the Icelandic documents are the Elder and the Younger Edda. The former is a collection of mythic and heroic poems, undoubtedly fragments of the songs that were preserved in the schools of the priests of heathendom. And here it is proper to suggest that the Celts described by Cæsar in his *Commentaries on the Gallic War* were not of the same race as the present Irish, Welsh, &c., but a Teutonic tribe. The present inhabitants of Bretagne are not descendants of the ancient Gauls, but are immigrants into France from Great Britain. Cæsar gives us a glimpse of the manner in which mythological songs and epics were preserved in ancient times in his description of the Druids. He tells us that the literature in their keeping was so extensive that it required twenty years to commit it to memory! This militates against the theory that the Eddic poems were folk-songs, that is, known by the whole people. That interesting passage in Cæsar describing the Druids opens to us a world of information. It gives us in a few striking sentences the key to the mystery in regard to the preservation in oral form, through many centuries, of the Vedas, the Iliad and Odyssey, the Niblung story, Beowulf, &c., and the Elder Edda. How and when the Elder Edda was recorded with Roman characters is a subordinate question. Whether it was gathered from the lips of persons who yet remembered fragments of the old Druidic songs of the north and put into a skin-book by the priest Sæmund Sigfusson, who died in the year

1133, or by some other Icelander, is an interesting but not important question. Even so great a scholar as the Swede Erik Gustaf Geijer contends that the Elder Edda existed in Runic before it appeared in Roman characters. Scarcely less important is the Younger Edda, said to be written by Snorre Sturleson, the great author of Heimskringla, who died in 1241. This work gives in prose form, with here and there a poetic quotation, a succinct account of the Odinic religion from the creation to the destruction and regeneration of the world. Some of the stanzas quoted are not recorded in the Elder Edda.

The Heimskringla, completed by Snorre Sturleson about the year 1230, contains a vast amount of information about Scandinavian heathendom, for it gives an elaborate account of the introduction of Christianity in Norway, portraying the conflict between the old and the new religion, and begins with sketches of a number of kings, who ruled Norway for one hundred and forty years before the introduction of Christianity. Hence valuable information may be found in that work, not only of the rites and ceremonies prescribed by the Odinic ritual, but also of the morals and habits inculcated and produced by the Odinic code. Several Icelandic Sagas are also of value in this respect.

The value of Cæsar has been indicated. With him ranks Tacitus. In the other Roman and Greek writers there is but little to be gleaned in regard to Teutonic mythology. Next after Cæsar and Tacitus came the Christian writers down through the foggy and dark Middle Ages, who, instead of writing in German or English (Anglo-Saxon) or other vernaculars, took to scribbling in Latin; but the very small amount of mythological information contained in their books is due in part to their ignorance, but mainly to their hostility to the heathen religion. Among this class of writers the North presents a remarkable exception in Saxo Grammaticus, who lived in Denmark in the 12th century. He wrote a *Historia Danica* and embodied it in an outline of Scandinavian mythology based on old songs. But he presents it as history, assuming Odin, Thor, and the other deities to have been kings and potentates in the North. The first eight books of his history are exclusively mythological. He has had a world of valuable light, though he himself saw nothing.

Finally the student of Scandinavian mythology must look for fragments of Odinism in the customs, habits, speech, traditions, ballads, folk-lore tales, and in the usages of the Christian Churches throughout Teutondom. The folk-lore tales are especially valuable, and during the last half century they have found splendid collectors in Germany (the brothers Grimm), in Norway (Asbjömsen and Moe), and in Iceland (Jón Arnason). These stories, like many of the ballads, are myths, in which the names of the gods have been changed or suppressed. The ballad and the folk-lore tale are the resurrection of the buried myth.

Scandinavian mythology and its relation to Biblical mythology is too vast a subject to be exhaustively treated in a magazine article. We shall simply give *in the next article, a brief synopsis*, condensed, as it were, under hydraulic pressure, and in the course of the narrative dwell more especially on those *features which have counterparts in Biblical theology*.

THE RELIGION OF THE ANCIENT SCANDINAVIANS.

X.

By the Hon. RASMUS B. ANDERSON.

WHERE the Scandinavian myth or doctrine is given, the reader must supply Biblical version from his memory.

> "It was Time's morning
> When Ymer lived;
> There was no sand, no sea,
> Nor cooling billows;
> Earth there was none,
> No lofty heaven,
> No spot of living green,
> Only a deep profound."

Thus the Elder Edda. The beginning was this: Many ages ere the earth was made there existed two worlds. Far to the north was Niflheim (the nebulous world), and far to the south was Muspelheim (the fire world). Between them was Ginungagap (the yawning gap). In the middle of Niflheim lay the spring Hvergelmer, and from it flowed twelve ice-cold streams called the Elivogs, of which Gjol was situated nearest Hel's gate. Muspelheim was so bright and hot that it burned and blazed, and could not be entered by those who did not have their home there. In the midst of this intense light and burning heat sat SURT, guarding its borders with a flaming sword in his hand. The Elivogs rivers flowed far from their spring-head in Hvergelmer into Ginungagap, and the venom they carried with them hardened, as does dross from a furnace, and became ice. Vapours gathered and froze to rime, and thus were formed in the yawning gap many layers of congealed vapour. But the south side of the abyss was lighted up by sparks from Muspelheim. Thus, while freezing cold and gathering gloom proceeded from Niflheim, the other side of the gulf was exposed to the dazzling radiance and scorching blasts of Muspelheim, and when the heated blasts met the frozen vapours it melted into drops, and *by the might of him who sent the heat,* these drops quickened into life and took the form of a giant man. His name was Ymer, and he became the progenitor of all the race of giants. At the same time, and in the same manner, sprang into life a cow, Audhumbla, by whose milk Ymer was nourished. The cow fed herself by licking the salt rime on the rocks, and at the end of the first day she produced by her licking the stones a man's hair, on the second evening a head, and on the third evening a perfect man. His name was Bure. He was fair, great, and mighty. He begat a son, by name Bor. Bor married the giantess Bestla, daughter of Bolthorn, and she bore him three sons, Odin, Vile, and Ve, and Odin became the father of the gods who rule heaven and earth. The three brothers, Odin, Vile, and Ve, slew the giant Ymer, and when he fell so much blood flowed that all the race of giants was drowned excepting Bergelmer and his wife, who escaped in a boat (ark) and perpetuated their race. The three sons of Bor dragged Ymer's body into Ginungagap, and out of it they made the world: of his flesh the land, of his blood the ocean, of his bones the rocks, of his hair the forests, of his skull the vaulted sky, which they decorated with red hot flakes from Muspelheim to serve as sun, moon, and stars. Ymer's brain they scattered in the air, and made of them the melancholy clouds. Dwarfs quickened like maggots in Ymer's flesh. But there were yet no human beings. One day Odin, Hœner, and Loder were walking by the sea and found two trees, an ash and an elm. They made of them the first man and woman. Odin gave them life and spirit, Hœner endowed them with reason and the power of motion, and Loder gave them blood, hearing, vision, and a fair complexion. The man they called Ask, and the woman Embla, and from them are descended the whole human family.

The counterparts of this story in Genesis need only to be mentioned. As a proof of the thoroughness, depth, and comprehensiveness of the old Scandinavian mind, the reader will note the fact that instead of making the world pass simply from chaos to cosmos, the old Scandinavians took a step farther back into primeval time, and conceived a *pre-chaotic* state (Muspelheim, Niflheim, and Ginungagap), then a chaotic epoch (Ymer, Audhumbla, Bure, Bor, Bestla, Bolthorn, Odin, Vile, and Ve), and finally cosmos made from the slain Ymer. The gods belonging to the Asgard Pantheon and also giants came into being in the middle or chaotic epoch. Odin was born in chaos. But the Scandinavian conceived living and lifegiving beings in the pre-chaotic age. SURT guarded Muspelheim before any creation or birth has taken place. Is not he the unknown god who is from everlasting to everlasting? SURT is also the last figure who appears in Ragnarok, the destruction of the world. He flings fire and flame over the world, and is the last one who appears in that terrible act of the drama. Elsewhere it is stated that Nidhug, a terrible serpent, dwells in Hvergelmer, in Niflheim. *Venom* flowed with the Elivogs rivers out of Hvergelmer. This points to an evil being in Niflheim, that is *from* everlasting, but after Ragnarok he sinks into the unfathomable abyss never to rise again, and thus he is not *to* everlasting. This dualism in the pre-chaotic epoch is a very interesting point in Scandinavian religion.

The Odinic pantheon has twelve gods to whom Divine worship is due, and there are twenty-six goddesses. The gods dwell in Asgard, but nearly every god has a separate dwelling. Thus Odin's high seat is Hlidsbjalf, whence he looks out upon all the nine worlds. He also has a large hall, the famous Valhal, whither he invites all men fallen in battle. Thor lives in Thrudvang, Balder in Briedablik, &c. Concerning the different gods, and particularly about Thor, Odin, Balder, and Frey, there are a number of beautiful myths, but it is not within the scope of this article to produce them here.

At once the most poetical and significant, the most lofty, beautiful, and impressive myth, is that of the great world tree, the ash Ygdrasil, the very name of which has its boughs laden with thought.

It is the tree of existence, the tree of life and knowledge, the tree of grief and fate, the tree of time and space; it is the tree of the universe. This tree has three roots, extending into the three principal worlds. The lowest strikes down into Niflheim, into the well Hvergelmer, where it is gnawed by the ancient dragon Nidhug, and all his reptile brood. The second root stretches into Jotunheim to the fountain of Mimer, where wisdom and wit lie hidden, and of whose waters Odin once purchased a draught, leaving one of his eyes as a pledge with Mimer. The third root is found in Asgard among the gods, near the sacred fountain of Urd, the norn of the past, where the gods sit in judgment, riding thither daily over the Bifrost bridge, that is the rainbow. At this fountain dwell the three norns, or fates, Urd (the Past), Verdande (the Present), and Skuld (the Future), and dispense the destinies of men. They do not spin the thread but weave the web of men's lives. They weave a web of golden thread from East to West, from the radiant dawn to the glowing sunset of man's horizon. The woof of this web is fixed in the dark North, but the web woven by Urd and Verdande is torn into pieces every evening by Skuld. The branches of Ygdrasil spread over the whole world, and aspire above heaven itself. An eagle is perched

on the topmost bough, and between his eyes a
hawk. A squirrel called Ratatosk runs up and
down the tree, seeking to cause strife between the
eagle and Nidhug. Four stags leap beneath its
branches and feed on its buds. Five swans swim
in the Urd fountain, and everything placed therein
becomes as white as the film of an egg-shell. The
norns draw water from this spring, and with it
they sprinkle Ygdrasil in order that the boughs
may continue green in spite of the destructive
agencies that constantly assail it. Honey-dew
falls from Ygdrasil, and is food for the bees. Odin
hung nine nights on this tree, and offered himself
to himself. Ygdrasil is a grand myth, and grand
things have been said of it by Thomas Carlyle and
Karl Blind, to whose descriptions the reader is
referred.

It may be worth while to notice in passing the
frequent recurrence of the number *three* in Scandinavian mythology. There were originally *three*
worlds, Niflheim, Muspelheim, and Ginungagap;
there were *three* stages of development, the pre-
chaotic, chaotic, and cosmos. *Three* gods, Odin,
Vile, and Ve, created the world out of Ymer's
body. *Three* gods, Odin, Hœner, and Loder,
created the first human pair. Ygdrasil has *three*
roots, stretching into *three* worlds, and these three

worlds are each divided into three subdivisions or sub-worlds, that is nine, which is *three* times *three*. There are *three* norns, three fountains, Hvergelmer's, Urd's, and Mimer's, and Odin hung *three* times *three* nights on the ash Ygdrasil, and several other recurrences of this sacred number might still be added before the list is complete. In the Bible we have the Father, Son, and Holy Ghost, while Odin, Vile, and Ve mean Spirit, Will, and Sanctity. Ve will readily be recognised as related to the German Wei in Weinacht (Christmas).

The development of the evil principle in Scandinavian mythology is scarcely less elaborately treated than in Biblical theology. How the dragon Nidhug and his brood originated in Hvergelmer that fountain Niflheim, and the probability that he existed from the time when primeval evolution took its beginning, has already been stated. The giant descendants of Ymer were evil, and they did not all perish in his blood-deluge, for Bergelmer and his household escaped like Noah of old, and like him produced a numerous offspring, with whom Thor and the other gods carried on constant war. But the great type or representation of evil is Loke. He is, indeed, the instigator of all the misfortunes that have happened both to gods and to men. He is of giant race, but was adopted by the gods, and was already in the dawn of time a foster-brother of Odin. He may not improperly be styled a fallen angel. The countenance of Loke is fair, but his disposition is thoroughly bad. It is an interesting fact that the Scandinavian mythology makes the devil good-looking and attractive instead of ugly-looking and repulsive. Why Christianity should represent the devil as the ugliest-looking being, and at the same time ascribe so much influence to him, is a mystery to say the least. Loke frequently accompanies the gods, and they make use of his strength and cunning, but when out of sight he usually plots with the giants for the purpose of bringing ruin upon the gods. He became the father of three terrible children in Jotunheim, that is to say, in the home of the giants. These are (1) the Fenriswolf, (2) the Midgard-serpent, also called Jormundgand, and (3) Hel, the goddess of death. The gods knew that these children of Loke were growing up and would some day cause them great mischief. Therefore they bound the Fenriswolf on a barren island and put a sword in his open stretched mouth, but for this the god Tyr had to sacrifice his right hand. They cast the Midgard-serpent into the deep sea, where he encircles the whole world and bites his own tail. Thor was at one time out fishing with the giant

Hymer. He caught the Midgard-serpent on his hook baited with a giant bull's head, and would have slain it with his hammer Mjolner, had it not been for the giant Hymer who got frightened and cut the fishing-line just at the moment when Thor had his hammer raised to strike. The third child of Loke, Hel, goddess of death, was thrown into Niflheim, and Odin commanded that all who died of sickness or old age should go to her; while warriors slain in battle were borne on valkyrian arms to Valhal. Hel's dwelling is called Helheim, and is large and terrible. Indeed her realm in the lower world is divided into nine regions one below the other, and it is in the lowest of these that her palace is called Anguish, her table Famine, the waiters Slowness and Delay, the threshold Precipice, and the bed Care. The English word *hell* is, of course, intimately connected with her name.

Loke caused the greatest sorrow to gods and men, when by his cunning he brought about the death of Balder. Balder is the most Christlike character in the Scandinavian mythology, and the account of his death has a strange similarity to that of the crucifixion of Christ. Balder was the favourite of all nature, of all the gods, and of men. He was the son of Odin and Frigg, and the Edda says that it may be truly said of him that he is the best god, and that all mankind are loud in his praise. So fair and dazzling is he in form and features that rays of light seem to issue from him, and we may form some idea of the beauty of his hair when we know that the whitest of all flowers is called Balder's brow. Balder is the mildest, the wisest, and the most eloquent of the gods, yet such is his nature that the judgment he has pronounced can never be altered. He dwells in the heavenly mansion called Breidablik (that is, broad-shining splendour) into which nothing unclean can enter.

Balder was tormented by terrible dreams indicating that his life was in danger. He communicated his dreams to his fellow-gods, who resolved to conjure all things animate and inanimate not to harm him, and accordingly Odin's wife Frigg, took an oath from all things that they would do Balder no harm. But still Odin felt anxious, and saddling his eight-footed horse Sleipner, he rode down to Niflheim, where he waked the vala or seeress, and compelled her to give him information about the fate of Balder. When it had been made known that all things had taken a solemn oath not to hurt Balder, it became a favourite pastime of the gods at their meetings to put him up as a mark and shoot at him. But it sorely vexed Loke to see that Balder was not hurt. So he took on the guise of an old woman, went to Frigg and asked her if all things had promised to spare Balder. From Frigg he learned that on account of its insignificance she had neglected to exact an oath from the mistletoe. So he straightway went and pulled this up, repaired to the place where the gods were assembled, and induced the blind god Hoder to throw the mistletoe at his brother and do him honour as did the other gods. Loke himself guided Hoder's hand. The twig did not miss its shining mark and Balder fell dead. The gods were struck speechless with terror. When they had had time to recover their senses, Frigg sent Hermod to the goddess Hel to ask her to permit Balder to return to Asgard. Hel said she would release Balder if it was true that he was so universally beloved, and this she would test by observing if all things would weep for him. Messengers were despatched throughout all the world to beseech all things to weep Balder out from Hel's domain. And all things did so with alacrity, men, animals, the earth, stones, trees, and metals, just as we see things weep when they come out of the frost into the warm air (a beautiful evidence that Balder is the sun or summer). The messengers were returning confident that their mission had been successful, but on their way home they found a hag crouching on the ground. She called herself

Thokk, but she was none else than Loke in disguise. Thokk said that she could not weep other than dry tears, and so Hel kept her prey. Now as Loke is physical heat and fire, Thokk's dry tears are the sparks that fly from the burning wood.

Soon afterwards Loke was captured and bound with strong cords to the points of rocks in a cavern. A serpent was suspended over him in such a manner that the venom fell into Loke's face drop by drop. But Sigyn, Loke's wife, took pity on him. She stands by him and receives the drops as they fall in a cup, which she empties as often as it is filled. But while she is emptying it, venom falls upon Loke's face, which makes him shriek with horror, and twist his body about so violently that the whole earth quakes, and thus earthquakes are produced. The relation of Loke to the devil, or Satan, in Biblical theology needs not to be pointed out.

But when Balder, the bright and good, had passed from the happy family circle of the gods, to the cold and gloomy abodes of Hel, the awful day of doom was impending. It was a fatal thing for the gods, and for the world, that they united themselves with the giant race. Adam and Eve should not have held intercourse with the wily serpent in the garden of Eden. The Norse gods should not have admitted Loke into Asgard. Christ's and Balder's death was the result, and this hastened the day when the whole world shall be destroyed, when gods, and men, and giants, shall perish in Ragnarok, the twilight of the gods. Increasing corruption and strife in the world are the signs that this great and awful event is impending. Continuous winters rage without any intervening summers now that Balder has been slain; the air is filled with violent storms, snow and darkness, and these are the signs that Ragnarok is at hand. The sun and moon are swallowed by giants who pursue them in the guise of wolves, and the heavens are stained with blood. The bright stars vanish, the earth trembles in the throes of the earthquake, and the mountains topple down with a tremendous crash. Then all chains and fetters are severed and the terrible Fenriswolf gets loose. The Midgard-serpent writhes in his giant rage and seeks land upon the tumultuous waves. Is not the reader forcibly reminded of passages in the New Testament, telling of the things that are to happen before the day of judgment? And does not this description suggest the fall of Troy? But what a serpent is this Scandinavian Jormungand, as compared with the two serpents that appeared before the burning of Troy, issuing from the sea, and casting their slimy coils around Laocoon and his two sons, and causing their death! But how much grander throughout, is not this Scandinavian Ragnarok than any other day of judgment ever conceived! The ship Naglfar, which has been built of the nail-parings of dead men, floats upon the waters carrying the army of frost-giants over the sea, and having the mighty giant Hrym as its helmsman. Loke, too, is now freed from his dark cave and strong chains, and comes to the scene as the leader of the hosts of Hel. The Fenriswolf advances and opens his enormous mouth. His lower jaw rests on the earth, and the upper touches the sky. It is only for want of room that he does not open his mouth still wider. Fire flashes from his mouth and nostrils. The Midgard-serpent placing himself by the side of the Fenriswolf vomits forth floods of venom that fill the air and the waters. In the midst of this confusion, crashing, and devastation, the heavens are rent in twain, and the sons of Muspel come riding down through the opening in brilliant battle array.

And now SURT, the same being that sent the heated blasts from Muspelheim into Ginungagap in the pre-chaotic world and by whose might the drops of venom sent by Nidhug in Niflheim quickened into the giant Ymer, he who is from everlasting to everlasting, this "unknown god" appears upon the scene, wrapped in flames of fire. His flaming sword outshines the sun himself. All the hosts here described come riding over the Bifrost bridge, that is the rainbow, which breaks beneath so great a weight. All this vast and glittering army direct their course to the great battle-field called Vigrid, and thus the giants on their part are ready for the final struggle.

Meanwhile Heimdal, on the part of the gods, blows his Gjallarhorn to arouse the gods, who assemble without delay. In his embarrassment Odin now, for the *third* time in his history, goes to the older race, that is, the giants, to seek advice. He rides to Mimer's fountain, where he in his youth had pawned his eye for knowledge, to consult Mimer as to how he and his warriors are to enter into action. The answer he received is nowhere recorded; but meanwhile the great ash Ygdrasil begins to quake and quiver, nor is there anything in heaven or on earth that does not fear and tremble in that awful hour. The gods and all the einherjes (*i.e.*, those men fallen in battle and brought to Valhal), don their armour, arm themselves, and speedily sally forth to the field of battle, led by

Odin, who is easily recognised by his golden helmet, resplendent cuirass, and his flashing spear Gungner. Odin places himself against the Fenriswolf as the foe most worthy of his steel. Thor stands by Odin's side, but can give him no assistance, as he must himself contend with the Midgard-serpent—and well matched they are. Frey encounters the mighty Surt himself, but though terrible blows are exchanged, Frey falls, and the Edda says he owes his defeat to the fact that he did not have that trusty sword which in his passion for a giantess he gave to his servant Skirner, when he sent him to ask the hand of the charming giantess Gerd. Thus it appears again and again that if the gods had not allowed themselves intercourse with the giants, they would not have come to this sad plight. In the last hour the dog Garm, which for ages had been chained in the Gnipa-cave, also breaks loose. He is the most terrible monster of all, and he attacks the one-handed Tyr, who had sacrificed his right hand in order to get the Fenriswolf bound. Garm and Tyr kill each other. Thor gains great renown by dealing the death-blow to the Midgard-serpent with his mighty hammer Mjolner, but he retreats only nine paces before he too falls dead, suffocated by the floods of venom which the expiring serpent vomits forth upon him. The Fenriswolf, with his enormous and wide-open mouth, swallows Odin; but Vidar, Odin's son, immediately advances to avenge his father. He places his foot upon the wolf's lower jaw, the other he seizes with his hand and thus tears and rends him till he dies. Vidar is able to do this, for he wears a shoe, for which materials have been gathered through all ages. It is made of scraps of leather cut off from the toes and heels in making patterns for shoes. Hence, says the Edda, shoemakers should throw away such pieces, if they desire to render assistance to the gods in the final conflict. Loke and Heimdal meet in duel and become each other's slayers. The conflict is still raging with unabated fury, when Surt, who is immortal, flings fire and flames over the world. Smoke wreathes up around the universal ash-tree Ygdrasil; the high flames play against the lurid heavens and the earth consumed sinks down beneath the watery waste. It is of course possible that this Edda account of Ragnarok contains elements borrowed from Biblical theology, but the fundamental elements are no doubt original, inasmuch as it is in perfect harmony with the Scandinavian system of mythology taken as a whole.

After Ragnarok comes a new world. The earth rises a second time from the sea, and is completely clothed in green. Sparkling cascades fall, overarched by rainbows glistening in the sunbeams. The eagle soars on lofty pinions in pursuit of his prey. The gods risen from the dead assemble on the Ida plains and talk about the strange things that have happened in the past, about the Fenris-wolf, about the Midgard-serpent, about Loke, and about the ancient runes of the mighty Odin. The fields unsown yield their bountiful harvests, all ills cease and the gods live in peace. A new sun, brighter and more resplendent than the former one, appears, and there is naught but beauty, plenty, and happiness. This pertains, however, only to the condition of the gods after Ragnarok; but what ideas did the ancient Scandinavians have of the future life of man? They had two heavens and two hells for humanity, a heaven and hell before Ragnarok and a heaven and hell after Ragnarok, the hell before Ragnarok corresponding somewhat to the doctrine of purgatory in the Roman Church. Before Ragnarok, those fallen by the sword or in battle went to Valhal to Odin, became einherjes who took part with Odin in the first conflict on the plain of Vigrid. Those who died a straw-death, that is to say, who did not fall in combat, went after death to the domain of Hel, and though the Edda is silent on the subject, they probably fought on the side of Loke in Ragnarok.

But after the twilight of the gods there is a heaven named Gimle and a hell called Nastrand. Gimle is a hall more radiant than the sun; it is the uppermost realm, and in it the virtuous shall dwell for ever and enjoy delights without end. Its description is brief but complete. Nastrand is the place set apart for the wicked. The word means strand of corpses. It is situated far from the sun, in the lowest region of the universe, is a large and terrible cave, the doors of which open only to the north. This cave is built of serpents wattled together, and the fanged heads of all the serpents turn into the cave, filling it with streams of venom in which perjurers, murderers, and adulterers have to wade. The suffering is more terrible than tongue can tell. Bloody hearts hang outside of the breasts of the damned; their faces are dyed in gore. Strong envenomed serpent fangs fiercely pierce their hearts; their hands are riveted together with red-hot stones. Their clothes though wrapped in flames are not consumed, and remorseless ravens keep tearing their eyes from their heads. From this terrible cave the damned are, to increase their anguish, washed by the venomous floods into Hvergelmer, that fearful well in Niflheim, where their souls and bodies are subjected to even more terrible pains and woes, torn by countless clusters of serpents, and borne from agony to agony on the whizzing plumage of the primeval Nidhug, the dragon of the uttermost darkness. The old Scandinavians did not believe in eternal punishment. There are passages in the Elder Edda that point to a final reconciliation between light and darkness, Balder and Hoder, between good and evil. There comes a mighty one to the great judgment and makes the dragon Nidhug sink. The vala or prophetess in her last vision in Voluspa points to a time when all that is evil shall be dissolved and washed away by the eternal streams of goodness. This is the last vision of the vala :

> "*There* comes the dark
> Dragon flying,
> The shining serpent
> From the Nida mountains
> In the deep.
> Over the plain he flies;
> Dead bodies he drags
> In his whizzing plumage.
> *Now must Nidhug sink.*"

There is an intermediate state, a transition, a purification, a purgatory in Hel's domain, and this object must sooner or later be accomplished, and the day of the great judgment, when *Nidhug must sink* and never more lift his wings loaded with suffering humanity, must come. The same idea is elaborated in Zendavesta. The Edda has it condensed in a single line, and does not Biblical theology tell us how great joy there is in heaven over a converted sinner? The Scandinavian like the Christian God is a God of mercy, who does not desire the eternal ruin of a single sinner but that he shall repent and live, and he is a god of omnipotence, who is able to press the tears of repentance from the heart though it be hard as adamant. He can dissolve all darkness and gild the world with the shining light of heaven. That Scandinavian mythology teaches an eternal reward is certain, and the view in regard to punishment as *not* being eternal is maintained by Scandinavia's greatest mythological student, the late learned N. M. Petersen.

And now a few words in partial recapitulation of the preceding pages.

1. There is a pre-chaotic world, in the south part of which, Muspelheim, Surt (the swarthy, dark, unknown) reigns with flaming sword, and in the north part of which Niflheim issues forth the venom-rivers, the Elivogs, indicating that Nidhug, the dragon in Hvergelmer, is co-eternal with Surt; that is, the good and the evil existed from everlasting.

2. Chaotic Ymer is produced by the blending

of cold and heat, fire and venom, sent forth into Ginungagap by Surt and Nidhug. Odin and the gods are the beneficent forces and elements in Nature. They separate themselves from the giants, which are the evil and destructive elements, and conquer them by their divine power.

3. Then comes Cosmos. Odin, Vile, and Ve create the present world from the body of the slain Ymer.

4. The government of the world is in the power of the Asgard gods, while they are more or less subject to the decrees of the mighty norns, the weird sisters, dispensers of time and fate. All that is good, beautiful, and true comes from the gods, but the giants also manifest their power in all the evil, disturbing, and destructive elements of Nature. The gods circumscribe but do not destroy the power of the giants. The world-life is a ceaseless struggle between these opposite forces. The gods strive to defend what advantage they have, but the giants are continually seeking to defeat them and bring ruin upon them. The gods frequently employ the giants to elevate and fortify themselves, but this is a mistake on their part, and they thereby only in the end weaken their own power. The cunning giant-god Loke, the devil or Mephistophiles of Scandinavian pagan-

ism whom the gods have adopted and taken into Asgard, deceives and destroys them. The power of the giants keeps increasing and grows more and more threatening to the gods and to the whole world.

5. In harmony with the doctrine of some Christian Churches, that wickedness is to increase until the last trumpet sounds, so in the Scandinavian religion the world grows worse and worse. It finally comes first to the death of Balder and then to the great struggle in Ragnarok, where both parties summon all their strength for a decisive battle, and where gods and giants mutually slay each other. In this internecine feud the world and the noble ash Ygdrasil are consumed with flames hurled by the mysterious Surt, that is, by the same original power whence came the first sparks of life in the pre-chaotic world.

6. The world is destroyed only to rise again in a more glorious condition. In the reconstruction and regeneration of the world the victory of the gods over the giants is complete. After Ragnarok, Odin, Thor, Frey, &c., are no more as individual divinities, but they are all united in that supreme being, that one who is greater than Odin, the one whom Hyndla's lay in the Elder Edda dare not name, and whom few look far enough to see—that

god who is dimly discerned in the primeval beginning, who remains victorious in Ragnarok, and who is from everlasting to everlasting. When that mighty one comes to the great judgment, then the cursed Nidhug, the gnawer in the dark, who has so long tormented the souls of the wicked, sinks, together with death and all pain and evil, into the unfathomable abyss never to rise again. Such was in brief the religion that fostered the enterprising spirit of the grand Viking age in the North. It is not unworthy of a modest place beside the other systems of heathen religions. It certainly inspired the ancient Scandinavians to live an upright and brave life. It has many "broken lights" of Christianity in it. The similarity in many parts only makes us wonder how it grew. Anyhow it saves us from having a low idea of the character of our rude ancestors.

POSITIVISM AS A RELIGION.

XI.

By the Rev. Professor J. RADFORD THOMSON, M.A.,
New College, London.

THERE is a curious irony in the fact, which will be for ever memorable, that the man who was the very incarnation of the scientific and secular spirit of the nineteenth century is yet the inventor of the only new religion to which (with the odd exception of Mormonism) this century has given birth. M. Comte was the author of Positivism, which is the doctrine that we have to do only with facts coming under exact observation, and with generalisations from those facts, *i.e.*, with physical "laws" deriving their authority from experience. Such facts and generalisations constitute, according to Comtism—which in this simply fixes and formulates a tendency of our times—the sum of human knowledge. Evidently the natural and proper outcome of Positivism is the negation of religion, for the doctrines of religion and its practices relate to the supersensible, the spiritual, the Divine.

Yet there is a Positivist religion, the "Religion of Humanity," with a creed, a church, a priesthood, a ritual, more or less developed and concrete. How can we account for a religion being tacked on to a scientific doctrine which seems to preclude its possibility? or illogically evolved out of such a doctrine? There is a general answer, viz., that men must and will have a religion, that it is not in human nature to be satisfied without a religion. And there is a special answer, viz., that the founder of Positivism became himself dissatisfied with his own secularism.

Comte must have imposed upon himself when he referred to his own experience the saying of Alfred de Vigny—"Qu'est ce qu'une grande vie? Une pensée de la jeunesse réalisée par l'âge." (What is a great life? A thought of youth, realised, made actual, in after-life.) No man's life was ever more clearly cleft into two distinct and antagonistic portions than was that of Comte. M. Littré was the most illustrious disciple of the great Positivist in his first and scientific stage—in that stage when metaphysics and theology were repudiated. But Littré broke off from the master when he publicly approved and advocated political absolutism, when he taught a fanciful doctrine of the Trinity, when he practised and sanctioned prayer. Many of Comte's followers "walked no more with him" when he became dissatisfied with those secular and negative doctrines which were so specially distinctive of the earlier part of his philosophic career. Thus we have two distinct parties, giving two distinct representations of Comte's personal history, two distinct views of the "chief end of man:" both parties, however, claiming to be expositors of Positivism. The reader of Robinet has quite a different impression of the master from that received by the reader of Littré. The former glorifies Comte as the founder of the true religion, and exalts "Ste. Clotilde" to highest honour, whilst painting the conduct of Madame Comte and of M. Littré in the darkest colours. To the great lexicographer, on the other hand, the later years of Comte seem to have been blighted by an irrational and infatuated forsaking of true science for false religion. "M. Comte," says Littré, "at a given moment, believing that he was simply developing the Positive philosophy, changed his method. The two sections of his teaching were manifestly two distinct doctrines, having different and irreconcilable points of departure. He exchanged the objective for the subjective method." Mysticism, in Littré's judgment, became the dominant influence, as his career approached its close. Amongst other points of divergence, Littré lays stress upon Comte's contention that the intellect ought to be subject to the heart, and that feeling, &c., should be attributed to the material world—a dogma which is naturally deemed a return from the Positive to the Theological stage of belief.

The best known English Positivists are warmly in sympathy with Comte's religious teaching. Thus Mr. F. Harrison claims that Positivism "belongs in the true sense of that word to the spiritual, and not to the materialistic philosophy," and even holds that "the scope, function, and parts of religion have never been completely examined until this was done by the founder of Positivism."

There can be no question that in his later years Comte insisted with reiteration and with earnestness that religion was the crown of his philosophic edifice. From his "Eight Circulars" we quote the following sentences in confirmation of this statement:—"Having devoted the whole of my life to the task of basing sound philosophy, and, as a consequence, true religion, upon the whole body of the sciences," &c. "Positive philosophy originates in real science, only that it may end in true religion." "It is in the Positive religion alone that resides the systematic force which can keep in check, not only the retrograde inclinations of the various governments, but the anarchical tendencies of their populations, prescribing simultaneously order in the name of progress, and progress in the name of order."

It is not always understood that Positivism, in its full development, is far more than a scientific method: it is a Religion and a Church. When Mr. R. Congreve, on the 19th of January 1859, inaugurated in London an ecclesiastical organisation he expressly affirmed:—"We are not a philosophical school, but a Church. ... We worship humanity in and through her noblest servant and organ, Auguste Comte." It is very noticeable that both master and disciples have been anxious to maintain a kind of continuity with the Christian Church in its highly organised mediæval form. The system is designated *Human* Catholicism in contrast with *Roman* Catholicism. It is maintained that the future of religion lies between Romanism and Positivism. "The religion of the past is our real competitor. Beside it there is nothing in the field." Positivism has its Trinity —Humanity, the World, Space! The Comtist idea of religion is a combination of the Christian and the scientific. Thus Mr. F. Harrison says:—

"We acknowledge a religion, of which the creed shall be science, of which the Faith, Hope, Charity, shall be real, not transcendental; earthly, not heavenly—a religion, in a word, which is entirely human, in its evidences, in its purposes, in its sanctions and appeals."

In many particulars the system of Comte is copied from the old Catholicism. It has its Calendar, Festivals, and Saints' Days; its Sacraments and Priesthood. The intention of the founder was that his religion should penetrate the social life of mankind, meeting men, as Catholicism aims at doing, at every point. Little has been done towards realising these plans; the temples, which are to be turned, not towards the East, but towards Paris, have yet to be built, the elaborate order of priests has yet to be instituted, the Pantheon has yet to be founded.

It is true that some distinguished men who have come under Comte's influence as a scientific thinker have refused to accept his religious teaching. M. Littré in France, and Mr. J. S. Mill and Mr. G. H. Lewes in England, may be mentioned as occupying this position. Those who take this position have Positivist tendencies, but reject the master's later and cherished doctrines; for them Comte is an authority in scientific method, but a fanatic in religion; they will follow his philosophy, but will have nothing to do with his Church. On the other hand, Dr. Bridges "accepts the conception of an organised Spiritual power, of a Positivist Church." He explains:—"For us the religion of humanity means something that will bind together all ages, all classes, and all nations, in a common faith and a common worship. We recognise the need, too, of something analogous to the spiritual authority which has directed the faith and the worship of all previous religions; and which, often as it has abused its power, has far more often used it beneficially and nobly."

Dismissing from our attention the one-sided Comtists, let us consider the beliefs and practices inculcated by Comte himself, and acknowledged by his thorough-going disciples to be authoritatively binding upon themselves. The religion prescribed by Comte is the religion of humanity; it substitutes for a Supreme Creator and Ruler the human race, or rather those members of the human race who by their character and services have deserved general esteem. The great and good of past generations are regarded by the Positivists with religious reverence, and are exalted to the position rather of deities than of saints.

In place of the "lords many and gods many"

who have so long usurped the throne of the human heart—in place of the Living and Eternal Supreme Himself—the prophet of the new religion bids us adore humanity as the sovereign and only deity.

Extinctis Diis, Deoque, successit Humanitas. By humanity, according to Comte's final definition, we are to understand "the unbroken whole of converging beings" (l'ensemble continu des êtres convergents). And as the majority of the human race, and almost all who have made a reputation for great services, are numbered among the hosts of the departed, we must form our conception of humanity by studying the character of those who have gone before us. "The fundamental principle of human order is this:—the living are essentially and increasingly governed by the dead."

It is not an easy thing to grasp clearly the Comtist conception of humanity as the deity whom we are called upon to worship. There is vagueness about Comte's own language:—"Towards humanity, who is for us the only true great being, we, the conscious elements of whom she is composed, shall henceforth direct every aspect of our life, individual or collective. Our thoughts will be devoted to the knowledge of humanity, our affections to her love, our actions to her service." Nor do we gain much in clearness by pondering the language of Comte's English disciple, Mr. F. Harrison:—"The entire system of Positive belief points to the existence of a single dominant power, whose real and incontestable attributes appeal directly to the affections in no less measure than they appeal directly to the intellect."

Such, however, is the Positivist object of adoration. "Under the permanent inspiration of universal love, the business of doctrine, worship, and discipline is to study, to honour, and to serve the Great Being, the crown of all human existence." To make the worship more real and profitable, the faithful are encouraged to personify humanity. Especially in private worship, *woman* is to be adored. A man should offer worship to his mother, his wife, his daughter. Comte himself adored as personifications of humanity his mother, his friend Clotilde de Vaux, and his estimable female housekeeper. An English Positivist asks:—"What is the most universal constituent of this composite spirituality? The answer is clear. It is in woman that we find it; and therefore it is that, as the most universal and the most powerful of all modifying agents, woman is, in our religion, the representative of humanity."

Comte was in the habit of writing in the most

extravagant terms of the person to whose influence he attributed his "moral regeneration." Thus, after the death of Clotilde de Vaux, he referred in one of his circulars to his place of abode in the following language:—"Especially sacred did this dwelling become to me . . . as the scene of the moral regeneration I experienced during one unparalleled year under the angelic impulse which will preside over the whole of my second life. . . . These holy walls, on which is imprinted for ever the image I adore, have helped me in my daily development of the private worship of the best personification of the true Great Being."

And in the dedication to Clotilde's memory of his *Positive Polity*, Comte confesses:—"As has ever been the case where affection has been well bestowed, your strengthening influence has spontaneously made me more affectionate to my friends, more indulgent to my enemies, more gentle to my inferiors, more submissive to those above me." Such language is by no means unreasonable; but Comte attributed to Clotilde's influence far more than moral improvement. He traced to this source the final development, which was indeed almost a reversal, of his whole system:—"Through you alone it is that I have been able to stir that reaction of the heart upon the intellect without which my mission would have failed. But for your gentle influence my long philosophic training, even though seconded by æsthetic pursuits, could not have enabled me to realise the true systematic preponderance of universal love, the principal and final characteristic of Positivism, and which more than any other will ensure its general acceptance."

As to what constitutes *worship*, we find a divergence of opinion prevalent among adherents of the Positivist faith. We do not find complete harmony between some of the fervid exhortations of Mr. Congreve and some of the commonplace, everyday sentiments expressed by Mr. Harrison. According to the latter, "Cult does not mean worship, but whatever stimulates the sense of duty and quickens the noblest emotions." Upon this showing, the Positivist θρησκεία takes the form of commemoration of great musicians, as Mozart and Beethoven, or of "the noble and healthful mediæval practice of pilgrimages or visits to the graves of distinguished men," such as Bacon, Harvey, Milton, Hampden, Cromwell, and William of Orange. One is reminded of the famous passage in the Apocrypha commencing with the sonorous invitation, "Let us now praise famous men, and our fathers which begat us!"

Comte felt the necessity of embodying the new faith in a living and social form, of investing it with the permanent attraction of ritual, sacraments, and various prescribed observances. Thus in the preface to the *Positive Polity* he contends:—" By this series of institutions (*i.e.*, the worship of guardian angels, and the sacraments), Proved religion shows itself capable of superseding Revealed religion at all points, depriving the latter of its claims to moral no less than to political superiority."

Religion, however, is not only a worship, it is a moral power exercised over human life. The best moral characteristic of the Positivist religion is that unselfishness and devotedness to human welfare which it has borrowed from Christianity. One of its advocates professes:—"In the principle of all action for the disciples of our religion—sacrifice of self for the good of others, embodied in the great formula of Positive morality, *Live for others*—I find the one all-powerful compensation, at once for the evils of our condition and for the hopes we renounce." The followers of Comte are in the habit of pronouncing Christian morality especially selfish, of representing Christians as seeking their own good as the chief aim; and they contrast with this self-seeking the disinterestedness of their faith and prayers. But a little reflection will show that the Christian precept, "Thou shalt love thy neighbour *as thyself*," is a wiser, juster, and more effective rule.

There is incongruity between the confident and almost boastful claims of the Positivists and the actual progress which the sect has made after so many years of promulgation. They speak in sonorous language of "the majestic march of our religion," and of the "rapidity with which humanity is moving on her course towards her visible installation." Yet, although Mr. Congreve used this language at the opening of the year 1881, we find him on the following New Year's Day noticing the disappearance of one of the two Positivist centres in Paris, and that the one with which he was most in sympathy; and recording that *two* sacraments had been celebrated in London in the course of 1881, viz., one of initiation, and one of marriage! It has been admitted that outside of France and Britain the adherents of the Positivist religion can be reckoned only by units.

It is a pleasure to acknowledge what of good there is in the religion of humanity. No Christian can regard this singular development of the spirit of our age with unkindness or bitterness. In Comte himself there was so much of egotism, conceit, and bigotry, that it is not easy to do justice to his enthusiasm and benevolence. In theory he professed universal love and goodwill, and certainly in his later years he aimed at cherishing such affections and desires as are an ornament and glory of human nature. And one cannot but sympathise with his desire to elevate the higher affections of men to a just position, in his religion and in the daily practice of Positivists. The best known English Positivists command our respect, both by their protest against materialism in belief and secularism in practice, and also by their bold and constant advocacy of righteous, peaceful, and unselfish policy in the relations of civil and national life.

But our admiration of much in the teaching and the practical life of our Positivist neighbours does not blind us to the fact that what of good there is in them is owing almost entirely to the religion of Christ, which has entered into the structure of the society of which they form a part, nor does it blind us to the fact that the peculiarities of Positivist doctrine are in themselves indefensible and misleading.

In criticising the "Religion of Humanity" we encounter the difficulty arising from the origin of the system as a supplement to scientific Positivism.

It seems to us most unreasonable to exclude from religion the supramundane and omnipresent Power. Comte himself tells us that "Religion has *not* to do with that order which is higher and more comprehensive than humanity, and which science forbids us to personify." Here is a fundamental metaphysical difference between the Positivist and the Theist. The former admits that humanity does not account for the universe, or even for itself. And yet he will only look *around* upon the living, and *back* upon the dead, instead of looking *up* to the Almighty and Omniscient Being who is the source and reason of all existence. The religion of humanity goes too far for the scientist, who acknowledges only the phenomenal and experiential; it does not go far enough for the spiritual philosopher, not to say the Christian.

Accordingly, the Positivist deity is an abstraction, towards which we cannot feel those sentiments which go out towards a living, conscious, personal being. And when the Positivist undertakes, for practical purposes, to personify his humanity, he necessarily selects types characterised by human imperfection. It needs an overpowering imagination, nay, it needs the abnegation of reason, to render religious homage to the illustrious dead whose memory we revere, to the living women whose virtues we prize, but with whose infirmities we are familiar.

Only a Supreme and Perfect Object of worship can issue a law which deserves universal and unhesitating obedience, or can promulgate a gospel which shall bring joy and hope to all human hearts. The collective goodness and imperfections, wisdom and folly, of the past cannot furnish us with an authoritative rule of conduct, or with sufficient moral sanctions to secure obedience. And judging from the tone of such Positivist writers and moralists as George Eliot, there is offered by this earth-born creed no pardon for the past, no peace for the conscience, and therefore little inspiration for future self-denial and devotion, for the benefit of the poor, sinful, and sorrowful sons of men.

And as Positivism limits our survey within the contracted horizon of humanity, so does it fail to lift the veil from the future and the unseen. It yields one hope—the hope that every good man's work may be serviceable to the coming generations. But upon the destiny of the individual and of the race, it is dumb. Christianity, on the other hand, allows and encourages the inspiring hope that a good man's life shall be the seed of spiritual progress and happiness on earth. And it adds to this hope the glorious revelation of a "new heaven and a new earth wherein dwelleth righteousness," and lends to this glowing prospect the added charm which is connected with an assured, a conscious, a personal immortality.

XII.

By the Rev. W. Nicolson, M.A.

THE following thoughts are submitted as bearing upon the great religious questions of the present time; more particularly in relation to the rationalistic assumption, that all the religions rest on identical foundations, or grow out of the same root-principles of human nature. Hence, though some of the religions may appear nobler than the others, yet this is only in outward semblance or appearance, as all alike are developments on a purely natural basis of the religious principles, which, original or derived, are to be found in humanity. This position the writer of the following chapters entirely denies. This denial is based on the fact, that the Religions of Humanity *belong to very diverse stages in the history of mankind*, and their worth and value in relation to humanity depend essentially upon the stage to which they belong.

Three such stages are clearly inevitable, and will be readily recognised as actually existing platforms or *planes* in the life of mankind. Auguste Comte has told us about his religious, his metaphysical, and his positive stages; but these are manifestly artificial, and like other French theories, are too obviously made for the convenience of the writer. But that there is a natural, savage, purely animal, or elementary stage in the history of humanity is surely obvious enough. In it man is to be found before he arrives at the second, or *moral* stage, in which there grows out of the interaction of the moral relations of man to man, a moral platform or plane, in which men substantially civilised are bound together by a network of moral relations which they conform to, not compulsorily, but by the force of habit and the internal sense of moral obligation revealed in human nature. No doubt this moral plane, in actually existing communities, is rather in a state of growth or *becoming* than fully realised and perfect. We see this in the existence, in all communities, of a number of human beings who are held in subordination by external compulsion, or by physical restraint, whose obedience to moral law is consequently only partial and compulsory. And so long as this state of things exists—and it does exist even amongst the peoples most advanced in civilisation—we mark the imperfection of this moral platform of humanity, and are reminded of what Locke says, somewhat cynically, in his tractate on the "Conduct of the Understanding," that "man is capable of becoming a reasonable creature." Kant, the thinker of Königsberg, has done most, more especially in his ethical works, to glorify this phase of human nature as the highest manifestation of humanity. Yet no one has done more to reveal its imperfection, to show its essential earthliness of condition; that unless man can hope to raise himself above this moral plane and attain nearer to that ideal towards which it points; but to which on this side of time it can never reach, his position is a hopeless one, and the thinkers working on such premises have no alternative but to fall back on the pessimism of Schopenhauer and Hartmann.

The moral plane, however, we hold, necessarily implies a higher. The thinker to whom we have referred as doing so much to exalt the moral plane of humanity, has shown that we are justified in inferring from the facts of man's moral nature the existence of God and the immortality of the soul;

the former as the only means of uniting and reconciling man's striving to obey the inward law of duty with the external order of nature and her ongoings according to the law of cause and effect; the latter as postulating the continued existence of man's moral being, as the only guarantee of his being able to reach forward to the real aim and ideal of that being and the fulfilment of the law of duty.

But surely we cannot stop at these bare and vague abstractions. We are, as Kant has shown us, on the basis of *real* moral life and action in making these inferences, and on this basis we *must* go further and postulate the practicability of reaching the Chief Good—the aim and ideal of man's nature, both individually and socially. But if the individual aim be union with the Divine Nature (2 Peter i. 4), the social aim is nothing less than that *Civitas Dei*—the City of God which floated before the mind of Augustine and other great Christian thinkers. Now this reaching forward to become "partakers of the Divine Nature," to become "members of the general assembly and Church of the first-born," is a state of things which may be anticipated here, as the lives of multitudes of the best of men have shown; though it may only be perfected when we reach the Golden City in very deed and truth. This, then, is that third and highest plane of which we are in search—the plane of the *spiritual*. Man may not only be bound by a network of moral relationships to his fellow-men, and live from inward principle, apart from external compulsion, in obedience to the moral law written on the heart; but he may also rise to communion with the unseen; live now as realising the actual presence of God, and thus "look" not at the things which are seen, but at the things which are "not seen." And it is precisely this wonderful apprehension of the "powers of the world to come," which constitutes the spirituality of earth, and enables man to look forward to a still higher spiritual condition in the future.

The Apostle in Hebrews xii. anticipates such a lofty sociological development when he says (verse 22)—"Ye are come unto Mount Zion, and unto the city of the living God," &c. &c.; and we contend that he here describes the spiritual stage or plane as reached *now*, in anticipation; though it will only be fully attained in the spiritual life-relations of the future.

Now the religions of the world connect themselves with, and belong to, these successive stages or planes in the life and history of humanity. All the religions, save Christianity and the religion of

Israel, belong to the natural stage. They do so from their polytheistic character, and from their manifold contradictions to the higher moral relations of humanity. The religion of Israel is the only religion which closely approximates in its principles and relations to the moral plane. As a religion, it is fully in harmony with this plane.

It is not maintained that the moral relations of humanity depend upon religion, though naturally they are closely connected with it, and the religion may raise or degrade man ethically. Morality is inseparable from humanity, and inevitably emerges in a more or less perfect state from the relations of man to man as a social being. We believe that revealed ethics is as inconsequent as revealed logic, and that morality is not a religious product; although, as we have said, it is greatly affected by the character of the religion accepted by the community, whose morality is under consideration. Man, intellectual, moral, and religious, is no doubt an inseparable unity; but the moral and intellectual developments of his nature are not an outcome of the religious; any more than the religious man is derived from the intellectual or moral man. All three are original developments of humanity, and do not necessarily depend the one upon the other, although, as has been said, there is abundant interaction between these great original principles of human nature.

I. In nature-religions there is, first, identification with nature. Her impulses are in man's blood. He feels himself at one with nature. His appetites, passions, and desires are implanted by nature, and the gratification of them is natural. Hence while he feels the presence of Divine power, and the instinct of worship reveals itself in the depths of his spirit, he deifies the whole of nature around him, and mixes together the lowest and the highest. Such states of religious feeling, as we have seen, must needs rest upon a Pantheistic basis—viz., that the *all* by which he is surrounded is Divine, in all its varied forms and impulses. Hence the worship of Pan and Bacchus amongst the Greeks, and the surrender to wild and sensuous impulses as the outcome of the inspiration of the god. But in a second stage, the all resolves itself into a variety of tendencies and impulses. The thoughtful and rational elements took form under Pallas Athene; the gross and sensual impulses were under the patronage of Bacchus and Venus, and the worshipper could pass from the service of the one to that of the other without feeling much the presence of moral opposites, or realising the contradiction that was inherent in his life. But as man advanced in moral culture, these contradictions began to emerge, and endeavours were made to solve or remove them. This was partly attained in the Greek religion by the Monotheistic tendency, in which Zeus became the father of gods and men, by the expulsion of the immoral elements from his character, the reconciliation of the warring inhabitants of Olympus through his control and mediation, and thus a solution of the contradiction was in some measure reached. But still in all the heathen religions this reconciliation was far from complete. The dark shadow of arbitrary mindless Fate rested over the gods, as it rests in the form of an inevitable necessity over the naturalistic schemes of modern times. Presently, moreover, the childish character of the popular mythology became apparent, and it lost its hold over men's minds; while we see how in Rome the darker and gloomier systems of the East took hold of the human spirit. Man shrinks from the absolute emptiness of unbelief just as in the case of the scientific spiritists of our own time. Accordingly the asceticism of the East, the Mithras' mysteries, &c., were accepted, in the hope that they would afford some remedy for the darkness and emptiness within. In these circumstances, the nature-worship of former times fell into disrepute, and educated by philosophy and art, the ancients began, so far at least as the more cultured were concerned, to reject the nature-worship of their ancestors. The consolidation of the moral plane, through the ordered law and social order of Greek and Roman life, doubtless did much to contribute towards this. Men felt their religions to be beneath them, while they ought to be above them. Socrates did much, reasoning on the foundations of the moral plane, to determine what the characteristics of a moral religion must be. Especially do we see it in such dialogues as the *Euthyphro*, where Socrates analyses the popular ideas of morality to show their fallacy. The sacred is shown to be that which is sacred in itself; what is founded in right and justice, and it is shown that this must be agreeable to the gods because of its essential character. In the *Apology* again he appeals to conscience as the arbiter of right and wrong, and not to the gods. The heroism of morality is urged in the *Crito* and the *Phædo*, in the assertion by Socrates of the duty of following conscience at all hazards, even to the death. In the *Gorgias* the pursuit of the chief good—the *summum bonum* is brought before us. It is not too much to say that the moral dialogues of Plato are specially directed to the confirmation, completion, and establishment of that which we have named the moral plane—the moral ties and principles by which mankind are bound together.

II. A moral religion, therefore, of the characteristics of which we are now in search, must be a religion wholly in harmony with the moral plane. The elements of a moral belief are unfolded to us with marvellous acuteness in these dialogues to which we have just adverted. But what is the leading principle of these elements as set forth by Socrates? Undoubtedly that which he nicknamed his demon —the power within which taught him how to live. This is no other than the voice of conscience—the moral law within unconditionally commanding,— "the superior principle of reflection or conscience in every man," as Bishop Butler names it in his first sermon on Human Nature. Whatever deficiencies may exist in the Kantean ethics, there can be little doubt that their strong point lies in the vindication of the authority of conscience and its identification with the individual; his acceptance, so to speak, of the moral law as a *datum* of the consciousness, as the law of his own being unconditionally commanding, or what he otherwise expressed under the crabbed form of the categorical imperative. In this he agrees with our own great moralist, Bishop Butler, to whose expressions, indicative of the authority of conscience, we have just referred. Corresponding to this principle, the high place of power in a moral religion is the "Lord of the conscience." This has been called the "vicegerent," the "witness for God in man," and the expressions are not at all too strong. In this lies the burning point of the moral argument for the existence of God. It must be taken for granted that the Creator and Disposer of the universe is also the "Lord of the conscience," and thus only are the "chief good" and the "chief end" of man attainable. With this is closely connected the argument for the immortality of the soul, on the ground that man's moral action is not an absurdity; but that a holy life—a life in harmony with the dictates of morality—is practicable, and not a self-evident absurdity. The service of the Good will not be engaged in, if the aims and ends it brings before men are unattainable. Moreover, in the unity we have referred to, which we are bound to postulate between the Creator and Preserver and the "Lord of the conscience," we have another principle of a religion occupying the basis of the moral, viz., God is *One*. Subsequently, when we come to examine the spiritual plane, we shall see how the Trinity in the Godhead has to do with, and is equally natural to, the spiritual plane; as the assertion of the Divine Unity is essential to the moral platform. The moral, as we have seen, cannot rise from earth. It points doubtless to heaven, it lifts up the "Lord of the conscience" as the "God who made the heavens and the earth," but it has no means within itself of establishing such doctrines; they are postulates, or necessary inferences.

A third principle, in addition to the attributing to God of moral attributes, is that in a moral religion the service must also be moral. It can tolerate no outrages upon human or paternal feeling as, for example, the sacrifice of Iphigenia. It must also present none of those orgies or corruptions which we have seen to belong to the heathen religions. But, furthermore, the very aim and end of such a religion will be moral. It will seek the perfection of man according to moral principles, or in other words, as it has a conception of what men *ought* to be and *ought* to do, it can never rest satisfied until the ideal thus raised be fully realised.

III. Closely connected with each other, though apparently indeed in polar antagonism, are the twin conceptions of *Law* and *Freedom*. It is not too much to say that without these conceptions, morality, in what we have called the human sense of the term, could not exist. It might exist without doubt in the Spencerian sense of the term; for in that sense there is only to be considered the welfare of the animal, as individual and one of a herd; the practical rules for which in man and brute—if there be any difference between man and brute—are deductions from their natural history. In such a thoroughly external view it is more than doubtful whether the question of freedom can be raised in the case of man any more than in that of the brute—and the outcome must be a pure Necessitarianism. Law is an external thing, derived from the persistence of force, which, as we have seen, is all in all. Out of force, as a mere brute necessity—and the evolutionist first principle goes no further—it does not appear how we can reach either God or religion, in the sense in which they have been hitherto understood. But if we take the humanistic view, with which we were occupied, the case is different; moral liberty and law in close relation, but yet in polar opposition to each other, presently emerge. Law—the sense of obligation, the consciousness of duty—is the primary and central fact of the moral consciousness.

But closely allied to this, is the conception of moral liberty, without which also morality, in the human sense of the term, could not exist. There lies, however, at the bottom of this conception another, with which we shall again have occasion to deal. This is the conception, that man as a moral creature is not under a brute necessity; but an independent, self-responsible, moral being. He is not independent, of course, of the "Lord of the conscience," of the Being or Power who has constituted him what he is; but in connection with this principle of freedom, he has been constituted a responsible creature, and within the latitude of that responsibility, he is a morally independent being. He recognises the moral law as the root-principle of his own being, adopts it as the maxim of his life, and postulates conformity to it, as possible and practicable. This last is the Kantean conception of freedom as connected with the autonomous or self-lawed character of the will—the autonomy of the will, as the philosopher names it. In this sense there is a social as well as an individual autonomy; as when a free people through their chosen representatives, constitute the laws which are to rule the national life. Freedom has, however, been understood in another or Pelagian sense as the power to conform to the law of one's being, or to violate that law. There can be no doubt but that such a power exists in a moral being, but whether this view is to be designated *freedom* is more than doubtful. If we take the power to do what we will as equivalent to freedom—and this has been done by Jonathan Edwards and others—then in that sense a man is free to leap over a precipice. But such an act speedily ends his freedom as a living being. In like manner, it may be said that a man is free to violate the moral law—to go against the sense of obligation of which he is conscious. But in that case he adopts as a maxim a principle contrary to the law of his being, *i.e.*, the law of conscience, which is the authoritative guide of his life; delivers himself up to the dominion of his brute appetites and propensities, and thus destroys, so far as that act or series of acts is concerned, the various foundations of his own moral nature. He becomes, in Scriptural parlance, the bondman of sin, the slave of his propensities.

IV. Returning, however, to the central line of our discussion—the characteristics of a moral religion—the points which have just been elicited in reference to the opposite but related principles of liberty and law, will be seen to throw considerable light upon what these characteristics must be. We have seen that in a religion on the purely moral plane, there can only be *one* God—the Lord of the conscience. If man's moral action as a concrete fact, or series of facts, be rational, its aims attainable, and man's life be not a stark, staring absurdity, it postulates or takes for granted that the Lord of the conscience is He who made and rules the heavens and the earth; furthermore, that the continuation of existence necessary for the accomplishment of the aims of the moral law is a fact; in other words, that the soul is immortal.

Again, the reverence due to the Lord of the conscience, and the adoration or worship due to Him as the embodiment or expression of this reverence, are also fully in harmony with the moral plane which is the foundation of the kind of religion which we are considering. But we have further elicited, in connection with the conception of law and freedom, that a moral being, though a creature—that is, not the lord of the moral realm, but a subject within the same—is yet a moral being gifted with large powers of independent action; the law he obeys is made his *own* law, the fundamental principle of his being—self-responsible, that is, accountable to the tribunal of conscience within. Such a being cannot *morally* be coerced by a law of necessity or compulsion. He is subject to the power of duty, it is true; but this is not natural but moral compulsion; otherwise, what we call *obligation*. Hence while there may be rewards and punishments in such a state, these rather contemplate the raising of the moral beings within the moral realm to the full realisation of their position than constitute legitimate motives. They are disciplinary and preparatory rather than ultimate and final. They aim at raising the individual to his full dignity as a moral being, rather than as things to be sought or avoided in themselves. The only truly valid motive in a moral creature is conformity to the moral law as revealed in the conscience. Hence the relation of the Lord of the conscience, or the Supreme, in the realm of moral intelligents to the subjects of this realm is, and must remain, a moral relation; not a relation of force, compulsion, or despotic rule. By their adoption of the moral law as the maxim of their actions, they enter into a pact, as it were, the pact which binds together the whole realm of moral intelligents, and thus they approach the moral Ruler as a moral Being, though infinitely exalted above them, and He deals with them as beings who are, in some sense, kindred to Himself—constituted after His image. His whole relation to them is thus a moral relation. He deals with them as beings under moral law, in and for behoof of the full realisation of the aims of the moral law; and they reverence and worship Him under the same limitation, that the grand aim of a realm of moral intelligents may be fully realised—a kingdom of God established.

V. But we must not forget a peculiarity of the moral plane or platform—that it is an *earthly* condition. It points to a state beyond, as necessarily connected with the realisation of the moral law, but it does not follow that it can know much of that ultimate state; nor is it necessary, as we saw in regard to rewards and punishments, that the nature of this ultimate state of being should be very fully revealed. Enough, that the moral law in its majesty, is revealed as the supreme rule of life; enough, that it is embodied in the Sovereign of moral intelligents; enough, that we should be fully assured that the ultimate aim and end of the moral law will and must be attained.

VI. Finally, we add a corollary which arises out of what has been said on the whole. We have not said that the moral plane is an inference or deduction from the supposition of a Supreme Ruler of the conscience, or of the moral realm, and the life and worship in relation to Him which necessarily follows. No; on the contrary, the constitution of such a moral plane in which man is related to man as moral beings, may be said to be, as we have seen in the previous part of our discussion, a natural necessity; the forces of man's life conspire together to its evolution or establishment; when established, the constitution of a moral religion with the characteristics we have been discussing, arises as a necessity of reason.

VII. We shall indeed see, as this earth cannot be our final home, that the moral implies a stage or plane beyond itself, in which its aims are fully attained, and in which the kingdom of God which morality can only proclaim as "at hand" is fully realised; "where the tabernacle of God shall be with men, and He will dwell with them, and they shall be His people, and God Himself shall be with them, and be their God" (Revelation xxi. 3, 4).

XIII.

By the Rev. W. NICOLSON, M.A.

THE utterance of our Lord, "'Η σωτηρία ἐκ τῶν Ἰουδαίων ἐστίν" (John iv. 22), spoken to the woman of Samaria, has a deep religious significance. It does not proclaim that religion is of the Jews, but that salvation (ἡ σωτηρία) is of the Jews. The nature-religions were not unknown to our Lord. In Galilee, where He spent His youth, there was much of the old Syrian nature-worship extant; while the Greek and Roman cults had found some acceptance, which they could not receive amongst the stricter and better-taught people of Judæa. There was thus, apart from that divine penetration which belonged to our Lord, the possibility of His having had some experience as to the relative position of the religion of Israel when compared with the heathen religions. The result of this was expressed in the sentence at the head of this chapter — "Salvation is of the Jews." Let us endeavour to consider what the meaning of this may be.

(2.) The reference can be only to one thing, the salvation to accomplish which Jesus Christ had come into the world. He came "to seek and to *save* the lost." That salvation which Jesus came to work out was life. "Strait is the gate, and narrow is the way," says our Lord elsewhere, "which leadeth unto *life*." The kingdom of God which He came to set up, which He already realised in His own consciousness, was therefore a kingdom of life. But was this life already revealed in the religion of Israel, so that when our Lord declared, that "salvation was of the Jews," it implied that they already possessed this life which was the substance of the salvation? This last question we must answer in the negative, for the Master says elsewhere, "I am the Way, the Truth, and the Life;" but if the life were already revealed, how could Jesus reveal it? yea, *be* it in His own person? To answer adequately this question we must remember the character of the religion of Israel, as repeated in its whole history. It was a religion of promise, which grew clearer and brighter as the ages rolled onward. To Abraham it was a promise that in his seed all the nations of the earth were to be blessed; to David, that of his seed One would appear who should sit eternally on His throne. To prophet after prophet came the message of life or salvation through a deliverer. In the sublime language of Isaiah : "Incline your ear, and come unto Me: hear, and your soul shall LIVE; and I will make an everlasting covenant with you, even the sure mercies of David." The religion of Israel was completely foreshadowed by the life of its first founder, the Father of the faithful and the friend of God. He came out of his own country, led by promise, the promise of the inheritance, which was, moreover, a promise not only for himself, but for his posterity. The patriarch entered into a covenant with God of future blessing to be realised by his descendants. And as age after age passed away, that history was but a history of decline from, and repeated renewal of this covenant of future blessing to be bestowed by God.

(3.) Now this covenanted character of the religion of Israel has very much to do with the specially moral or ethical character which as a religion we have attributed to it. Kant, the philosopher, to whom on a variety of occasions we have referred, speaks somewhat contemptuously of the religion of Israel (see *Religion innerhalb der Grenzen der blossen Vernunft, III Stück, Zweite Abtheilung*).

But this only proves that the philosopher, like Homer, sometimes nodded; and his English translator, noticing his agreement with Bishop Warburton, remarks, in reference to the philosopher's observations as to the absence from the religion of Israel of the sanctions of a state of future retribution, that here he not only contradicts Warburton but himself. His latest German editor and commentator, Herr Kirchmann, calls this part of his work *dürftig*, that is to say, *poor*, and we fear that it fully deserves the designation. He has some remarks about the impotence of compulsory laws as influencing the conscience, which are true, but have been carefully ignored by the Government of his own country, who have all but extirpated[1] the Christian religion, by putting it under the management and direction of the police.

But it is surely curious, when we find the following observations from the philosopher, " Da nun ohne Glauben an ein künftiges Leben gar keine Religion gedacht werden kann, so enthält das Judenthum, als ein solches in seiner Reinigkeit genommen, gar keinen Religionsglauben,"—" Since with-

---

[1] This language may be regarded as too strong by some of our readers; but we submit, when the church attendance in a great capital falls to 1 per cent. and a fraction, as admitted in a paper recently read before the Evangelical Alliance, the Christian religion is certainly in a fair way towards extirpation.

out faith in a future life no religion can be thought to exist, and since Judaism as a religion strictly considered does not contain such, it cannot be considered as a religious faith." We know of another religion, viz., the religion within the bounds of reason, excogitated by a certain philosopher, to which the same objection applies. But he adds further : " It is scarcely to be doubted that the Jews, like others, even the rudest of peoples, must have had not only faith in a future life, but also, of course, *as a heaven and a hell;* FOR THIS FAITH, *in virtue of the universal moral constitution of human nature, comes to every one as a necessary thing.*" Most true, Mr. Philosopher, but there are reasons for everything ; and just as there are reasons for the *very feeble mention of a future life* in your religion within the bounds of bare reason, so there are better reasons still for its seeming omission in the religion of Israel. But before coming to this point, it is desirable to notice more fully how important the covenanted character of the religion of Israel is, as bearing upon what we have said respecting it, as the only religion on the moral plane, or on the ground of the moral, which has ever existed. We have already noticed, as brought up by the German philosopher, the danger of making religion a thing of the police.

But the philosopher has failed to notice, that while in some sense the religion of Israel was, as an external polity, and bound up with national law, necessarily a compulsory religion, there was another sense, and a higher one, in which it was not compulsory at all. This was in its relation to God. The heathen religions set forth gods, whose hateful tyranny was in violent contradiction to the highest parts of our common nature. It is in relation to this that De Quincey has said, that the Roman must have had, on occasions, a strong desire to kick Jupiter, his supreme god. We know, moreover, that savage peoples are addicted to chastising their gods. But this was just because their gods were no gods in accordance with the moral sense of humanity, but deifications, in virtue of the instinct of worship, of the arbitrary forces of nature. But morally, as we have seen, the case must stand otherwise. We have remarked (p. 208), " He— *i.e.*, the worshipper on the basis of morality— is not independent of the " Lord of the conscience," of the Being or Power who has constituted him what he is; but in connection with the principle of freedom, he has been constituted a responsible creature, and within the latitude of that responsibility he is a morally independent being. He recognises the moral law as the root principle of his own nature, adopts it as the maxim of his life, and postulates conformity to it as both possible and practicable." We saw, further, how under moral law, and on the moral plane, the Lord of the conscience, whom we are compelled to regard as the God who "made the heavens and the earth," and sustains them, places man in regard to Himself on purely moral relations. Now this is entirely the case with the religion of Israel. Jehovah, the covenant God, places Abraham and his descendants on purely moral grounds and relations in regard to Himself. He binds Himself by the same law under which He places them; He is bound entirely by the terms of the covenant as much as they are, yea, in a far higher and deeper sense, for as a perfectly holy Being He cannot deny Himself, but is bound by His own covenant, whether the other party to it adheres to its terms or not. Do the severe judgments of Jehovah in dealing with His people in regard to their lapses from the covenant in any way invalidate this? No doubt, as we have seen, the grand legitimate motive on the moral plane, is reverence of and obedience to the moral law, as commanding unconditionally. But still a state of preparation, as in the family, and discipline so as to raise those under the law to the full understanding of it and its requirements, may be recognised. The religion of Israel was full of injunctions as to this instructory process in regard to the families of Israel; and the rewards and judgments which were offered to Israel, whom Jehovah names His son, may be regarded, and are commonly regarded, as a disciplinary process to raise him fully up to the requirements of the moral law. The rewards are subsidiary motives, appealing to man's desire for happiness, as are also the punishments inflicted for violation of the law. These rewards and punishments do not destroy Israel's freedom, do not violate in any way his position as morally related to Jehovah, nor does Jehovah step out of the moral character which belongs to Him in inflicting them.

(4.) The ceremonial law is to be regarded in like manner as a disciplinary process, having the same end in view as the rewards and punishments of which we have just spoken. Israel was to be like his God—"Be ye holy, for I am holy;" and the ceremonial law was an elaborate teaching by facts and symbols of the necessity of holiness. Even the cleanliness and purity which were enjoined, were calculated to impress upon Israel the supreme importance of purity of life and heart. The religion of Israel has been accused of externalism, and no doubt it is in some degree open to the reproach; but we see how, in the last of the TEN WORDS or commands, the law points to the lust conceived within as the source of the outward transgression, and seeks to confront and check evil in its first inception in the heart. But this was more fully provided for, in the personal relation of the individual Israelite to his God. He was more than the gods of the heathen, which stood in a general or collective relation only to the whole people, but had less to do with the individual. It was not so with the God of Israel. As "searching the heart and trying the reins of the children of men" (Jer. xvii. 10), He stood in closest *personal* relation to the individual Israelite, and He invited not only the fear, but the love of His people, though as founded upon law, as preeminently a moral system, fear seems to preponderate over love. "The fear of the Lord is the beginning of wisdom." If the Israelite turned to the earliest records of his people, he could read the familiar and even tender relations in which the first founder of his people stood to Jehovah. Abraham was the friend of God, admitted to a tender and gracious intimacy; and the same was true of Isaac and Jacob, of Moses, and others of the patriarchs. This warm and close relation of affection and reverence, in which the Israelite was invited to come in regard to Jehovah, must bring out streams of spiritual life, and we have only to turn to the Psalms and Prophets to see how fully and splendidly this was verified. What deep breathings of upward aspiration! "As the hart panteth after the water brooks, so panteth my soul after Thee, O God. My soul thirsteth for God, for the living God: when shall I come and appear before God?" (Psalm xlii.) And what religion, save the unique spiritual religion of the world—Christianity—can parallel the tender joy and confidence of the twenty-third Psalm—"The Lord is my Shepherd; I shall not want. He maketh me to lie down in green pastures: He leadeth me beside the still waters. He restoreth my soul: He leadeth me in the paths of righteousness for His name's sake. Yea, though I walk through the valley of the shadow of death, I will fear no evil: for Thou art with me; Thy rod and Thy staff they comfort me. Thou preparest a table before me in the presence of mine enemies: Thou anointest my head with oil; my cup runneth over. Surely goodness and mercy shall follow me all the days of my life: and I will dwell in the house of the Lord for ever." There was thus abundant preparation and means for the cultivation of personal religion in the religion of Israel; and personal religion must be ever a thing of the heart and life. It was indeed here that the religion of Israel rose above its natural level and anticipated Christianity. Here the Israelitish religion was not only a moral, but became by anticipation a spiritual religion, just as the child is the father of the man; and we may perceive the lower level of development foreshadowing the higher.

(5.) For while there was in Israel those streams of spiritual life still preserved to us in the Prophets and Psalms, yet Israel, nevertheless, as a people, remained essentially on the moral basis. The law was its watchword, and even their piety and religious life were restricted and confined by the law. And this not merely the law as an external, objective thing, but mainly by the law given within, the law of the mind warring against the appetites and passions,—the law of sin in the members, yet often succumbing to them, and having abundant reason to cry out, as the apostle does — "Oh, wretched man that I am, who shall deliver me from the body of this death?" The basis of the moral plane is the *sense of obligation*, the moral law given as a *datum* of the consciousness. The law of conscience is the centre of man's moral being, but still it is a *law*, an abstraction, which presses on the man with unyielding power, and commands unconditionally, no doubt, but has in the reverence which it awakens in the heart only an imperfect spring of obedience. The conflict arises within the personality which the apostle has so graphically described in the seventh of Romans, with the sad result, that the "law which was ordained to life, is found to be unto death" (Rom. vii. 10).

The externally given law, written not on the fleshy tables of the heart, but on tables of stone, only intensified the struggle. It was the reflex of the law written on the heart, graven, as it were, on the rock, and holding up objectively the law of conscience in defiance of all attempts to tamper with, or warp, or silence the inward voice within. And the result both as described by the apostle in the chapter just referred to, as obtaining in the heart of the individual, and as exemplified in a larger scale in the history of the Israelitish people, was to show how imperfect and insufficient the purely moral basis is in itself. In regard to Christianity—the temptation under which is to fall back on the moral basis, as the temptation of Israel was to fall back on the natural basis and the nature-religions—there is good reason for the prejudice of the pious mind against what it describes as mere "cold" morality. No doubt there may be perversions of spirituality, as there are perversions of morality. But the prejudice referred to is well founded, because it recognises the essentially earthly and insufficing character of the purely moral stage. We have already pointed to these in dealing with the view which regards morality as a humanistic and self-sufficing thing. We saw how this view was especially represented in the ethical doctrines of Kant, and how the tendency was to evaporate what seemed the sound and stable foundations of the edifice into mere abstract notions or ideas. The lord of the conscience need only be an idea. As a critic justly remarks of the relations of religion to this view of morality, that she, *i.e.*, Religion, "was merely called in to be a sort of dry-nurse to morality, for she must do duty generally for this when in a weakly condition; but so soon as morality gets a little stronger upon her legs, she shows religion to the door!"[1] But while the recognition of morality as all-sufficient leads to this, we see it also exemplified in the history of Israel, whose religion, ultimately at least, occupied a purely moral basis. The law was its watchword, and the result was, as we have seen, alike unsatisfactory in the individual and in the nation. The final result

---

[1] O. Pfleiderer's *Die Religion, ihr Wesen und ihre Geschichte*, vol. i. p. 16.

in the history of Israel was the creation of the Pharisee. Now what is the Pharisee? Not merely the name applied to a canting, hypocritical religionist, for it would be calumny to say that the Pharisees were all such; the Pharisee is one who consciously and with full purpose sets about making himself better, and who, while ignorant of the deepest evils of his own heart, is consciously growing in self-esteem and self-satisfaction through his supposed victorious advance in truth and righteousness. Says Bunyan, as he passed through this stage: "And for a whole year I thought I pleased God as well as any man in England." Israel occupied essentially the moral stage; the law of God to be wrought out and exemplified in its minutest details, its "mint and its cumin," was her boast and her constant aim; while in victorious advancement in self-conscious external, and especially *ceremonial* morality, and holding the law as a national badge, she at the same time forgot the inward principles of truth and righteousness.

(6.) We shall see that the supposed hiatus in the religion of Israel, as to the doctrine of the future life, arose from the very circumstances on which we have been treating, viz., that Israel's religion, as a people, was on the purely moral basis. Systems of ethics have, as a rule, little to say about a future life; they occupy themselves in developing the moral relations between man and man as denizens of earth, and although they may rise to the recognition of a Supreme Being, they can only speak of man's relations to Him as a creature, and under moral government here on earth. Such was also the case with Israel. Recognising Jehovah as the national God, the Ruler of Israel, in covenanted relations with whom as a people they "lived, moved, and had their being," from whom they had received the promise of "life, breath, and all things," it was not surprising that they found this to be final and sufficing. The ancients were as yet destitute of that conception with which we are so familiar—the conception of eternity, duration unregulated by that conception of time which, together with space, is said necessarily to form part of the furniture of our perceiving faculty. In the Psalms the devout Israelite felt himself in the hand of that God who was so near to him, who "had been the dwelling-place of his fathers in all generations," and he was content to leave himself in His hands without straining his eyes to catch some glimpses of the world beyond the grave. In the twenty-third Psalm, while he rejoices in the sense of Jehovah's nearness, goodness, and mercy, he says—"Goodness and mercy shall follow me all the days of my life; and I will dwell in the house of the Lord for length of days," as the concluding words of the psalm are translated in the margin of our English Bible. The pious Israelite felt so joyful and blessed and safe in the hand of Jehovah, that he was content not to be too curious about the future. The mystery of life and death presses most heavily upon the speculative, the sceptical, and the unhappy. The soul who can trust God with its future is less anxious about it.

(7.) But finally, a comparative inquiry as to the position of the religion of Israel in this respect, as compared with the highest of the nature-religions, or even with Islam, which has been classed with the religion of Israel, as occupying with it the same moral platform. We have ventured to say that the religion of Israel is the only purely moral religion extant, as Christianity is the only spiritual: let us now endeavour to make good this position as regards the first of these. Our would-be advanced thinkers look down from their lofty critical standpoint and speak of "the religions," as they pass them in review, as if they all occupied the same place and had the same relations to the human consciousness. We affirm, on the contrary, that there is in reality no comparison, for in the whole course of the world's history only one purely moral religion has appeared—the religion of Israel; and at the fulness of the time only one spiritual religion— the religion of Jesus Christ.

(8.) We have seen what the characteristics of a moral religion must be. They are, that God is the Lord of the conscience, that He is necessarily *one*, and that His worship and service must be, in harmony with His position as the Lord of the conscience, entirely moral in their character. But furthermore, morality implies freedom; that man's obedience to the law should be a free and not a compulsory, slavish obedience. As an external national polity, there were some aspects of the religion of Israel in which it was necessarily compulsory, but in the highest of all aspects it was free. Jehovah had entered into covenant relations with His people, and was as much, nay, truly more fully bound by the terms of the covenant than Israel itself. We saw, further, how the externalism of the Israelitish religion was corrected by the tender and intimate relations to God into which the devout Israelite might enter, the result of which is the living fountains of spiritual life which we find in the Prophets and Psalms.

Finally, in the fact that Israel was, at least in the first ages of his national existence, so satisfied with his trust and confidence in Jehovah as the national

God, which it was his privilege to exercise, that there was seemingly little or no inquiry about the future life, which Kant takes to be a necessary article in any true and genuine religion. In the first place, time, future time, was only thought of indefinitely as *secula seculorum*, to use the Roman expression; and secondly, as we have seen, the pious Israelite was brought so near to his God, was able so to confide all into His hands, that in the sense of the presence of Jehovah, and in the enjoyment of the blessings granted to him, he was contented to trust Him as to his future. No doubt, in the great calamities which clouded the fall of Israel, the future life and the doctrine of the resurrection began to occupy a more prominent place, but not till then. Here, then, we have all the marks of a genuine *moral* religion — in its necessarily strict monotheism, and in the moral character of its worship, which the recognised system of rewards and punishments, and the observation of the ceremonial law shows to be imperfect, indeed, but not self-contradictory. How, for example, does the Iranian or Persian religion, which otherwise bears so noble a character, stand in comparison with the Israelitish? How does the religion of Buddha or Sakya Muni? These religions are below the moral level—the religion of Zarathrustra, because, not to speak of its dualism, and the high place given to Ahriman, it recognises other gods besides Ahuramazda. He as supreme god recognises Mithra, as so high, that it was said he himself brought sacrifices to him. Besides Mithra, whose mysteries came into vogue in the later days of Rome, we read of the god Craosha, the companion of Mithra, and indeed the whole of the circle of the ancient Persian gods was strangely taken up and accommodated to his system by Zarathrustra—a strange contrast to the inward worship and the means of attaining to virtue, of "the pure sentiment, the true word, and the good act."

Buddhism, with much to recommend it to the acceptance of men, especially in that Indian world where it found its home, occupies morally even a less honourable position than the religion of Zarathrustra. It is defiled by taking up the whole Indian Pantheon into its heaven, though it subjects them to Buddha, or the wise man. This, however, as has been shown, is not absolutely new; for in Brahmanism the wise man, in virtue of his prayers, may become the master of the gods, and use them as the puppets of his pleasure. Again, the essence of evil in Buddhism is nothing else than existence itself, the destruction of which under the torments of the endless transformations of the metempsychosis is the very corner-stone of the system. Some have admired the moral precepts which are to be found in Buddhism; but more or less of morality is associated with all forms of religion. The truth is, God has written the moral law so deeply on the heart of man, that even when called in question by the pantheist, or denied by the atheist, it still vindicates its authority and power. It was thus, as the Apostle Paul tells us, that the Gentiles "did by nature the things contained in the law;" thus showing the "work of the law to be written on their hearts." And hence, the presence of morality under the sway of a certain religion is no indication of the moral tendency of the religion itself. There is morality in all religions. As we have already seen, nature, if we may so speak, conspires to moralise mankind, and to render complete and stable that moral *plane* or platform to whose existence we have drawn attention. We have but to remember how, under the Greek and Roman mythologies, with their fairy-like Olympus, through the corrective influence of a settled order and civilisation, such a high moral condition was reached, that the Greek and Roman philosophers could discuss most of those questions and moral problems which we sum together under the name of ethics; and in considering this state of things, we perceive that men may advance in the practice and theory of virtue, not because of, but in spite of their religion. Still there can be no doubt that a religion in the course of centuries greatly modifies and raises or degrades the character, morally, of the people who profess it. Now, if we apply this to the religions under discussion, we shall see how they operate in their influence upon the character of the people who professed them. We have already dwelt upon some of the defects of the religion of Israel, defects arising from its being a preparatory rather than a final religion, and arising also from the fact that it rose but little above the moral plane, and partook consequently of the defects of morality, as a merely earthly, inchoative, and imperfect system. The defects culminated in its latter days in Pharisaism, or an intensely self-conscious, self-exalting, and at the same time barren legalism; into Saduceeism, or the scepticism and infidelity of the privileged classes, whose business it was, as classes, to administer the religion; and finally into monasticism in the religion of the Essenes, who, as in the case of all monastics, give up the struggle with the world for the establishment of the kingdom of God, and fleeing to the desert or the monastery, seek to save themselves from the common destruction! These evils arose, however, in the last days of the religion of Israel, not because there was any contradiction or inconsistency in the religion of Israel as regards the principles of morality; but because the Jewish people, instead of cultivating the spiritual element which was inherent in their religion, and which was developed to great fulness in the spiritual life of the devouter part of the nation, the expression of which we have preserved in the prophetic and poetic books of the Old Testament scriptures, adhered but too rigidly to the purely moral basis, and thus sank into a barren legalism and formalism, in which the Jew rests to the present day.

(9.) When, however, we turn to Buddhism, the case is different. There are grave inconsistencies and contradictions in the system in relation to the moral plane of the life of humanity. First of all, a truly moral religion can only recognise *one* God. Buddhism took up the whole Hindoo pantheon, though it placed its gods in a powerless condition in relation to Buddha. "My power is great," Brahma, the supreme Indian god, is made to say in a Buddhistic legend; "but what can I do against a priest of Buddha?" Again, morality is human; it seeks to perfect human life, not to destroy it. But the Buddhistic morality, with all the commendable things in it, has this defect, that it seeks not to develop and perfect, but to destroy. This is seen in its monasticism, with its nihilistic and pessimistic character, its endeavours to destroy and not to perfect humanity. No doubt the Buddhistic system has effectually tamed the rude Mongols, but its results are everywhere negative rather than positive. It seeks to tame, to empty, yea, in truth to annihilate humanity. And these passive, self-emptying virtues are only practised on the lower levels of the system; when we come to the higher, then its negative and nihilistic phases become all too apparent. They aim them not only at taming the passions and subduing the lusts, but at the destruction of self-conscious existence, the quenching and extinction of the human spirit. It speaks of love of being, and establishes hospitals for vermin; it esteems life so sacred that it will not kill the vermin on its own body; but, as Max Duncker, the historian of antiquity, remarks—"Love in the system of Buddha is not as in Christianity, the highest commandment for its own sake, not, as in this, a liberating, active, and creative ethical power, which not only negatively seeks to uproot selfishness, but strives also to cause the natural man to be born again into the moral[1] condition; the love of Buddhism, on the contrary, lamenting the universal lot of conscious being, seeks to render

---

[1] More properly the spiritual.

the community of life a little more endurable. Love is thus to the Buddhist essentially only a means to soften and diminish the universal suffering of living beings." And, as we have seen, this ceases in the higher stages of the system; the self-regarding quietism which then sets in, regards only self, sinks into self-contemplation, or more properly, endeavour after self-annihilation. True morality has ever an ideal, both ethical and practical, in the lord of the conscience and the kingdom of God; Buddhism knows neither of the two—its ideals are only earthly Buddhas, its practical aim self-extinction. One who has lately written on the state of the Mongols, amongst whom this religion is all-prevalent, remarks on the helpless, hopeless condition to which their religion has reduced them—their willing submission to the most grinding despotism, their apathy in the path of improvement, and their dependence for the arts of life on their Chinese master.[1]

(10.) But finally, we have the Buddhistic paradise, the state called Nirvana. This has awakened much controversy, and has been variously considered in Europe of late, and, indeed, in the systems of Schopenhauer and Hartmann we have a kind of intellectual Buddhism, arising and becoming the

[1] See Gilmour's "Among the Mongols," chap. xviii. pp. 210-243.

most popular philosophy of the time, in the midst of the culture and enlightenment of the Fatherland. In our own country, the charms and glories of Buddhism has kindled the muse of Mr. Edwin Arnold in his " Light of Asia." But what is Nirvana? The blackness of annihilation has been covered with poetical images, as flowers and wreaths are cast on the tomb, and men are made to believe that—

> "Only when all the dross of sin is quit,
> Only when life dies like a white flame spent,
> Death dies along with it,"

as if there were in some sort a life in death in the midst of the blank darkness of the Buddhist Nirvana. It is doubtless true, and for good reason, that Sakya Muni refused to pronounce that Nirvana was extinction, as he also refused to affirm that it was life. This was probably a prudent reserve. Even the votary who would flee the endless wanderings of the metempsychosis might still shudder at the blankness of annihilation!

> "Sad care! for who would lose,
> Though full of pain, this intellectual being!
> These thoughts that wander through eternity."[1]

But that Nirvana is annihilation, blank extinction, no one can doubt who studies the whole tendency of the system? Existence itself is evil, and this,

---

[1] See Milton's "Paradise Lost," Book II.

according to Sakya Muni, must be destroyed. Passion, feeling, desire, every movement of the spirit must cease, and absolute rest from the evils of existence must be obtained. But is the longing after immortality still to remain? There is to be absolute cessation from all aspiration, yearning, longing of every kind, and yet the longing after immortality in the blank darkness of Nirvana is still to remain? This is flat contradiction, and therefore we hold that Herr Oldenberg, in his lately published able work on Buddhism, has shown the fallacy of Professor Max Müller's reasoning when he would, mainly on abstract grounds, convert the nothingness of Buddhism into a positive state of eternal felicity! "If we follow," says Herr Oldenberg, "the dialectical consequence, there can nothing be looked for than a blank vacuum." And identifying, further, "Ego," "Self," and "Person" the Buddhistic texts, he remarks: "It seems clear in enough that both words are different names for the same concept, and that he who denies the existence of 'Person' cannot maintain the existence of the 'Ego' as more than a mere possibility."[1]

Such is Buddhism, with its existence—a hell to be cooled in some measure by the mutual aid of the unhappy victims; its highest life, the extinction of

[1] See Oldenberg's "Buddha," ss. 273 ff.

all feeling and thought; its paradise, annihilation; its final result, a blank atheism.

(11.) There remains yet that we should look briefly at the pretensions of Islam as a moral religion. Much of it, no doubt, is a syncretism drawn from Christian and Jewish sources. The most emphatic doctrine of Islam is the affirmation of the unity of God, and here its superiority over the corrupt forces of Christianity and the heathen Arab superstitions it supplanted cannot be doubted. In this respect it rises superior to the popular forms of Eastern Christianity to the present day, whose image and picture worship amount, in the case of the common people, to actual idolatry, the images being named gods. In this respect the appearance of Islam has been a powerful protest for the unity of the Godhead. But side by side with this we have the doctrine of *kismet,* or fate, which has exercised, and continues to exercise, such an evil effect upon the Mohammedan nations to the present day. This is not the doctrine of predestination, such as is to be found amongst Christians, but the ancient doctrine of an irresponsible fate made a part of the Mohammedan religion. The sensuality and fleshly lust which Islam allows, nay, takes up into its paradise, are in conflict with the laws of morality; so much so, that the Mohammedan mystics are themselves ashamed of them, and endeavour to explain them away. The Mohammedan paradise with its houris; its polygamy; its rooted sanction of slavery; its approval of war even for missionary purposes, are all in conflict with an enlightened morality, and amount in many cases to a degradation of humanity. Especially is this marked in the universal degradation of the female part of humanity, and the consequent corruption of the family, and the evil results to education and the advancement of the race.

Amongst Christian nations war is waged in despite of Christianity,—it is taken up and adopted as part and parcel of Islam. Finally, the institution of slavery as sanctioned by Mohammedanism is a degradation of humanity. No doubt polygamy and slavery were permitted also in Israel, but they were limited by such restraints, that they were almost extruded from the national life, and certainly never had those evil influences they have had upon the Mohammedan nations.

(12.) The final conclusion to which we come is, then, that although the religion of Israel was provisional, and, moreover, the religion of a people in a rude state of society, and exposed to the constant inroads of foreign foes, yet it is by far the highest of all the religions of the ancient or modern worlds, always excepting Christianity, of which it may be regarded as the precursor. We have insisted upon its coincidence with the moral level of humanity, its full acceptance and development of moral freedom, its strict monotheism, and the principle of life and growth in it arising from its close and gracious relation to Jehovah, out of which grew and were nourished the noblest men and women of the nation.

In relation to Jehovah, women were placed upon an equality with the rougher sex, and were often the vehicles of the revelations of the Divine will, as we see in the case of Deborah the prophetess and others. That in some points Israel fell below the moral level, with which it was generally coincident, is explained by our Lord as arising from the imperfect and rude state of the Israelites, as in a state of religious growth and progressive advancement. But the moral stage, as we have seen, is only itself an imperfect state. The Religion of Israel was not and could not be final, for the kingdom of God, which it presupposed, and which formed its ultimate aim, with its higher level of spirituality, was destined to supersede it. Our final conclusion is, that this religion was the only one that has closely approximated to the moral plane of humanity.

A word in conclusion as to the higher level taken

by Christianity—as the unique *spiritual* religion. This lay in the actual coming of the kingdom of God. That kingdom was first embodied in Jesus Christ, as the second Adam; whose pure consciousness reflected back and was in entire harmony with the divine life of the Father; and His life was to illuminate "every man coming into the world." The organon of this higher plane is not the sense of moral obligation as on the lower planes, but *faith*, as the vision of "things not seen" and "the foundation of things hoped for." The subjects of this kingdom are no longer servants, as under the ancient covenant, but children, "heirs of God and joint heirs with Christ." In them, Humanity, newly created and joined to its Head, is to partake of, and to be raised, in ever approximating union, to the Divine Nature, to the throne of God.[1]

[1] 2 Peter i. 4; 1 John iii. 2; Rev. iii. 21.

www.ingramcontent.com/pod-product-compliance
Lightning Source LLC
Chambersburg PA
CBHW021408230426
43666CB00006B/673